I, Soldier

A VOICE FROM THE AMERICAN CIVIL WAR

Drew W. Allbritten

HELLGATE PRESS ASHLAND, OREGON

I, Soldier

I, SOLDIER
©2024 Drew W. Allbritten

Published by Hellgate Press
(An imprint of L&R Publishing, LLC)

Drew William Allbritten asserts his moral right to be identified as the author of this original work. All rights are reserved without limiting the rights under the copyright owner above. No part of this publication shall be reproduced, stored in or introduced into a retrieval system, or transmitted in any form or by any means (electronic, mechanical, photocopying, recording or otherwise), without the prior written permission of the copyright owner.

Hellgate Press
Ashland, OR 97520
email: sales@hellgatepress.com

Interior & Cover Design: L. Redding

All photos courtesy of the Library of Congress/National Archives, except the following: Pages viii, 3, 100, 125, which are from the author's private collection.

Library of Congress Cataloging-in-Publication data has been applied for.

ISBN: 978-1-954163-82-9

Printed and bound in the United States of America
First edition 10 9 8 7 6 5 4 3 2 1

A Soldier's Creed

I am an American Soldier.
I am a Warrior and member of a team.
I serve the people of the United States, and live the Army Values.
I always place the mission first.
I will never accept defeat.
I will never quit.
I will never leave a fallen comrade.
I am disciplined, physically and mentally tough, trained and proficient in my warrior tasks and drills.
I always maintain my arms, my equipment and myself.
I am an expert and I am a professional.
I stand ready to deploy, engage, and destroy the enemies of the United States of America, in close combat.
I am the guardian of freedom and the American way of life.
I am an American Soldier.

(Written by Members of the Task Force Soldier's Warrior Ethos Team, 2003)

I, Soldier

An Infantryman's Creed

I am the infantry.
I am my country's strength in war, her deterrence in peace.
I am the heart of the fight…wherever, whenever.
I carry America's faith against her enemies.
I am the Queen of Battle.
I am what my country expects me to be, the best trained
Soldier in the world.
In the race for victory, I am swift, determined, and
courageous, armed with a fierce will to win.
Never will I fail my country's trust.
Always I fight on…through the foe,
to the objective, to triumph overall.
If necessary, I will fight to the death.
By my steadfast courage, I have won more
than 200 years of freedom.
I yield not to weakness, to hunger, to cowardice,
to fatigue, to superior odds,
for I am mentally tough, physically strong,
and morally straight.
I forsake not my country, my mission,
my comrades, my sacred duty.
I am relentless.
I am always there, now and forever.
I am the infantry!
Follow me!.

(Written by Lt Col Stephen H. White in 1955. Adapted from a poem titled *I am the Guard* by an unknown author which was discovered in the Nation Guard Archives.)

Inventory of Contents

Foreword	*ix*
Dedications & Acknowledgments	*xi*
Prologue	*xiii*
Author's Notes	*xvi*

1861   1

1. Good-by Maw	3
2. Privates	5
3. Officers	6
4. Infantry Slang	7
5. Wagon Ride	8
6. Violets and Violence	8
7. Forgive Me	9
8. Dem Darkies	9
9. Over Time	10

1862   13

10. Been Better	14
11. Waitin' and Prayin'	14
12. New Recruits	15
13. Copperheads and Hookers	16
14. Ironclads Clash	17
15. The Unforgiven	18
16. Night Picket	19
17. Volunteer's Diary	20
18. Scavenger	26
19. Yours, But Not Ours	27

20. King Cotton	28
21. Stars or Bars	28

1863   31

22. Winter Battle	32
23. Glory or Death	33
24. Gettysburg Revisited	34
25. Drummers, Signallers, and Buglers	35
26. Elephants	36
27. Aftermath	37
28. Missing	37
29. Friendship	38
30. Music at 100 Paces	40
31. Bushwhacker	43
32. Heartbroken	43

1864   45

33. Sarah Jane	46
34. Blue Dogs	47
35. Home Guard	48
36. Skedaddle	50
37. Womenfolk	50
38. Willows	51
39. Tough Decisions	53
40. No Longer	54
41. Dice and Beer	54
42. Clara's Angels	55
43. Last Breath	56
44. Regimental Flag	57
45. Not Ready Yet	58

1865   61

46. What's in a Name   62
47. Gone Too Soon   62
48. Belle Boyd   63
49. Prison Camp   64
50. Hoping for a Tomorrow   66
51. All Equal Now   67
52. 100 Miles   68
53. Traitor   69
54. One Soldier's Prayer   69
55. Colored Troops   70
56. Lost Soul   71
57. Breeding Barn   71
58. Litter Bearers   73
59. Grand Review   74

SOLDIER RECOLLECTIONS   77

60. Jacob   78
61. Sooner or Later   85
62. Company Life   86
63. Comrades Reunite   88
64. Mathew or Matty   90
65. On Meeting Myself   96
66. Cornelius   96
67. To Love Again   101
68. I, Soldier   101

Epilogue: Picket and Potato-Peeler   *103*
About the Author   *127*

Foreword

Drew W. Allbritten was an American Civil War reenactor for nearly two decades. He creatively portrayed a young, semi-literate man from a small northern town who enlisted in the Union Army at the beginning of the Civil War.

Drew was involved in dozens of battle scenarios and in scores of living history events; and this collection of writings realistically describes the emotions, fears, tensions, and friendships of a soldier then (and perhaps even now).

While no reenactments can truly demonstrate the brutalities of war, this collection provides a unique glimpse into the perspectives and challenges of a typical Civil War private.

I, Soldier covers each year of the nation's Civil War with some reflections on the impact of those involved. Using authentic 1860's language and numerous photographs from the period, it seeks to take the reader into the 1860s by dramatically re-acquainting them with the American Civil War.

Decades ago, when the author was a young adolescent, his elderly great-grandfather told him about his own father who had fought in the Civil War and about some of his exploits.

So now, in these timeless and emphatic writings, one can truly visualize a homesick soldier leaning into flickering candlelight, and with an ink-stained pen nib or a shaven pencil stub, scrawling down recollections of his survival in dire circumstances. And as the late evening winds howled outside his smoke-filled tent, this anguished soldier could not sleep.

— Richard L. Anderson,
*Academy Award recipient (sound effects),
movie producer & screenwriter*

I, Soldier

On March 4, 1861, Abraham Lincoln was sworn in as the 16th President of the United States:

I, Abraham Lincoln, do solemnly swear that I will faithfully execute the Office of President of the United States, and will do the best of my ability, preserve, protect and defend the Constitution of the United States as registered in Heaven.

[In Article I, Section 2, Clause 1, The Constitution provides: "The President shall be Commander-in-Chief of the Army and Navy of the United States, and of the Militia of the several States, when called into the actual service of the United States...."]

On March 4, 1865, Abraham Lincoln was sworn in for a second term as President:

I, Abraham Lincoln, do solemnly swear that I have never voluntarily borne arms against the United States since I have been a citizen thereof; that I have voluntarily given no aid, countenance, council, or encouragement to persons engaged in armed hostility thereto; that I have neither sought nor accepted nor attempted to exercise the functions of any office whatever, under any authority or pretended authority in hostility to the United States, hostile or inimical thereto. And I do further swear that, to the best of my knowledge and ability, I will support and defend the Constitution of the United States against all enemies, foreign and domestic; that I will bear true faith and allegiance to the same; that I will take this obligation freely, without any mental reservation or purpose of evasion, and I will well and faithfully discharge the duties of the office on which I am about to enter, so help me God.

[Amended in 1862 by Congressional Statute to include an "Ironclad Test Oath" requiring all civilian and military officials to swear they had never aided or encouraged persons engaged in armed hostility against the United States.]

Dedication & Acknowledgments

This creative work is dedicated to all servicemembers of the United States Armed Forces who daily and faithfully keep their oath to solemnly swear to defend the American Constitution against all enemies foreign and domestic – and to their families. It is also dedicated to those historians, authors, and teachers of the American Civil War who continue to pursue the truth, and who relentless convey the reality of this terrible era accurately and forthrightly against the forces who would like to suppress their voices.

Creative writing is in many ways a team effort. I appreciate having the use of the public domain photographs that are held in the National Archives' Mathew Brady's Collection of Photographs of Civil War-Era Personalities and Scenes. I am indebted to the many people who offered encouragement, advice, expertise, and ideas on content and style. I sincerely thank the late William Allbritten, Richard L. Anderson, Alan Greenwald, Larry Harris Jr., Gregory Hawkins, Amalie Hill, Jacqueline Keefe, the late Michael Kelly, the late Robert Krueger, Christian Laine, Mark Lyles, George McKellar, Larrell Rittenhouse, Ronnie Smith, the late Matthew Urbanowicz, and Arthur Visser. I also acknowledge Harley B. Patrick, Owner and Publisher of L&R Publishing LLC and his team at Hellgate Press, who made this project a reality. And, first and foremost, my wife, Professor Susan Anne Kelly, who encouraged, pushed, and badgered me for years to be creative outside my professional bubble, thank you. Your practical and morale support kept me going.

Prologue

2021-2025 is the 160th anniversary of the American Civil War. Years ago, as a reenactor, I portrayed a typical Union soldier. I participated in over twenty-five different battlefield simulations and in scores of living history activities from 1981-1998 for the 125th, 130th, and 135th anniversary engagements of this tragic conflict.

As someone who worked in and around the nation's Capital for twenty-five years, and during that time, I served as a presidential appointee for seven years. I studied the history of this American tragedy and its personalities, primarily from the perspective of the everyday regular army soldier.

Like most other dedicated reenactors, I read numerous biographies of both Union and Confederate survivors. During these living history events, I made diary entries, and wrote letters and poems to loved ones as if I were living during that time: putting my thoughts into 1860s words about the emotions, fears, tensions, and friendships of a typical Civil War soldier. I took on the voice of a young, semi-literate man from a small northern farming community. In all, I wrote sixty-eight verses and vignettes.

I was motivated to go back to these writings when I watched on television the failed insurrection attempt at the nation's Capital on January 6, 2021. As Confederate flags flew in the Capitol building, and on its grounds, I was heart-broken. But not my spirit. Almost 160 years earlier, another insurrection surfaced when the Confederate artillery fired on Union soldiers at Fort Sumpter in Charlestown Harbor in South Carolina. And with the intense political polarization in U.S., now is the right time to publish this collection.

In the northern states, the Civil War was fought to preserve the Union and to end slavery. And it did. But not without great sacrifice and suffering, some of which continues today. In the southern states, this was a war to secede from the Union to preserve its way of life, its slavery, states' rights, and white male privilege. The Union won this bloody Civil War, but many others in these once-confederated states still seek to glorify their traitorous past.

To this day, American democracy is being challenged again, from the inside. My collection of verses and vignettes seeks to honor and to remember the pain of those soldiers and civilians, then and now. My hope is that this work will be a reminder to those fomenting rebellion in the nation today We only need to look at the Ukraine and Gaza to understand better the impact of modern warfare on a nation and its people.

Author's Notes

I, Soldier is a collection of verses and vignettes on one man's soldiering experience and insights, the experiences of his Union comrades, and the conversations overheard between Yankee and Rebel soldiers.

On cadence and rhyme: In the period around the Civil War, soldiers and civilians were familiar with what were known as *Parlor Ballads*, especially with the works of Stephen Foster. The stock in trade of a Parlor Balladeer was the rhyming couplet, or the rhyming of every line. This form of rhyme can sound sing-songy to the modern ear. In the interest of fidelity to the parlance and style of the era, I have used rhyming couplets in many of the verses in this work. *For greater effect, you can be the storyteller by reading the verses aloud.*

On grammar and punctuation: During the Civil War era, there was a wide range of oral and written language skills among the soldiers. Nearly all officers were much better educated than the soldiers they led. As a result, soldiers would often ask their literate comrades, officers included, to help them write their letters home.

The author chose to write in the voice of a semi-literate, but insightful private: informal and colloquial with poor and inconsistent phonetic spelling. Why? Because the vast majority of the Civil War soldiers – on both sides – were under-educated privates. Their stories, in their own words, have too often been lost, supplanted by reports of officers, journalists at the time, and historians later.

Photographs: Most of the photographs in this work were all in the public domain and many can be found in the National Archives' Collection of Mathew Brady's Photographs of Civil War-Era Personalities and Scenes. Other photos are from the Library of Congress or the author's private collection and all have received the necessary permissions.

I, Soldier

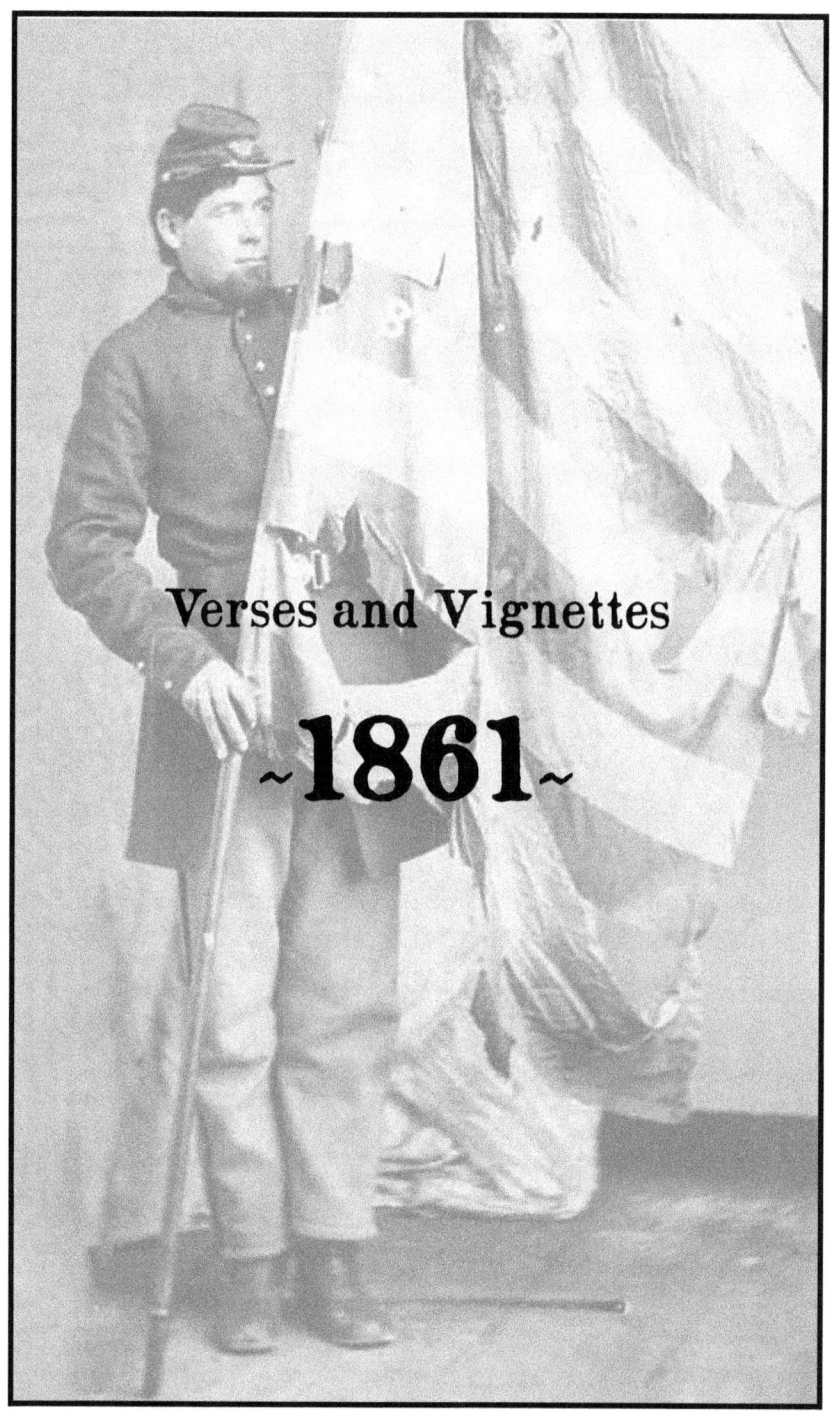

Verses and Vignettes
~1861~

1. GOOD-BY MAW

(Adapted from a WW1 enlistment song, "Long Boy," written by William Herschel.)

Good-by Maw, good-by Paw, and
  good-by mule wit yur ole hee-haw.
I may not be knowin wot dis war za bout,
  but you be sure I be soon findin out.
So, I be walkin on down to da town hall square,
  and be gettin in line wit de otha boys ther.

Yawl, don't be a fearin or be a frettin,
  I soon enuff be a homeward boundin.
S'pose I be shootin me som Rebs and ole Davis too,
  and dats bout all one fellar can do.
So, good-by Maw, good-by Paw, and
  good-by mule wit yur ole hee-haw.

2. PRIVATES

Fur a Private, tiz jest a fightin man's wurld,
  and be followin orders unda doze colors unfurled.
To fight dat able foe widout a given name,
  and bein courageous, widout acquirin ainy fame.

Fur a Private, da dirt twas hiz only bed.
  Not so great, but tiz bedder dan bein shot dead.
We recruits be dreamin of many a gloryus battle,
  but dem vetrans jest hope fur dry ground, all.

Fur a Private, he not yet be knowin true sorrow,
  and doze vets ar jest thankful fur anotha morrow.
Dailee, he be findin anotha place to bivouac,
  az days blend togetter, tiz hard keepin track.

Fur a Private, derz no chance fur a brevet.
  jest to march, eat, sleep, fight and sweat.
Da soldier mostlee be prayin fur dreams undashed.
  ev'n afta doze Blue 'n Grey ranks brutlee clashed.

Fur a Private, he oft be hearin doze words 'at all costs.'
  witch meanz dis battle will soon be lost.
Dis soldier caint ne'r be well-prepard to die.
  he jest be hopin to be one day mor unda de uncarin sky.

Fur a Private, at da cemetery, hiz family shall soon weep,
  whence dare son be takin hiz too earlee furev'r sleep.
Der be no medal fur valor on hiz sunken chest,
  only da patriotism buried deep widin hiz breast.

3. OFFICERS

Fur de Officer, derz only command and a yearnin fur gallantry.
   Perhaps whilst revivin an ole West Point rivalry.
Da officer hopes each bludee battle be not in vain.
   In battle dare iz so lil time fur ainy pleazur or pain.

Fur de Officer, derz many portant battlefront liaizons.
   Whilst hiz men follow hiz orders wit laden caissons.
Da officer oft longs fur hiz wife's lovin embrace.
   Den, off to a hero be, or to die wit God's grace.

Fur de Officer, he always tryin to be actin so brave.
   Hopin to be earnin a brevet, whilst avoidin da grave.
Da officer's men do be loyalee followin da flag, bugle and drum.
   Let dare be glory fur dem soldiers or be seein kingdom com.

Fur de Officer, dare must jest be victory afta victory.
   Since he be hopin to be footnoted in de writen history.
Dare will ne'r be peace unda dem American stars.
   Till doze 'Bars' and 'Old Glory' be mendin dare scars.

4. INFANTRY SLANG

(A conversation between a sargent and a new Union recruit.)

Private! Ar you a fresh fish recruit? And frum whence you com?

> Yessah, Furst Sargent! Sorry I dint salute ya fast nuff. I jest be comin frum Ohio.

I hope ya aint goin to be no shoddy, pie-eatin soldier. So wot ya doin rite now?

> I jest be learnin som new army words, like tar bucket, horse collar, and pepperbox. So wots da difrence tween a pie-eater or fresh fish? A new recruit, I spoze. So wots a copperhead or a scallywag? Wots a slebag or a satterlee? Sarge, wots da difrence tween quick-steppin or quick-marchin? Wots da difrence tween da abatis and da palisade? Or tween da barbette and da berm? I jest be gittin confused too easy. I be tryin not to be a contumacious miscreant at da van. Iz dat da frontlines? Wot do 'we be seein da elephant' mean? Som say it be meanin 'battle.' Dat right? I jest be learnin dat possum be meanin a good friend or comrade, and dat skunk be meanin a foe or jest ainy officer?

I be heppin ya later wit dat, Private. Wot you be gittin fur me now?

> Well, here goes. Be lookin like ar skirmishers jest be beatin dem begrimed grey lice. Doze yella skunk-led vermins sur be skedaddlin fast. In da van, I jest be losin my brogan, beehive, and Bowie toothpick. Will dat be costin me plenty greenbacks in my pay. Well, I gotta bit bloodied and soon be seeein de ole sawbones. Glad, I be not soon lyin in no wooden casket. So, I be grabin me a root and be eatin som goobers too, jest to be fillin up my growlin breadbasket. Dis better dan eatin doze moledee sheet iron crackers. But dey be hurtin my bedraggled choppers. I be hopin I wont be needin to be quick-steppin to dat smelly latrine. Now, fur som shut-eye capers. Dats it, Sarge!

Not bad, Private. You be makin me grin. Now, you jest be stayin alive. Yur dismissed.

5. WAGON RIDE

Death twas not som silent thief in de darkest of night,
 but ratter a voracious predator in broad daylight.
Why do Death be stealin de last breath of ainy single soul,
 whence it can be swallowin doze battalions whole?
Wot do a soldier be thinkin durin hiz very last breath?
 Will he soon be ridin on dis woeful wagon of death?
Jest God alone will ventualee be decidin
 wich soldiers be live-marchin or be dead-ridin.

6. VIOLETS AND VIOLENCE

Abuv doze violets purple derz som violence so vivid.
 De armies be clashin and twill later be honorin dare dead.
In dis once lush green valley of lilacs and clover,
 where doze valiant boys be vanishin in each maneuvre.

Abuv doze violets purple derz som violence so vivid.
 Dem fearless warriors bein filled wit uncertin dread.
Soon doze meadows wer littered wit mud-caked kepis,
 and neath doze fallen wer dem much-trampled pansies.

Abuv doze violets purple derz som violence so vivid.
 Mayhem's sad wake be now lookin like an unkept bed.
Az doze flattened violets becom da warriors final pillows,
 dis violence be now searchin fur mor floral hollows.

7. FORGIVE ME

I be havin da deepest pain fur dis proud soldier I be killin.
Twas to be him or be me. I be havin no choice. Lord, do be forgivin.
Thee be knowin dis fearless foe-man be havin a well-loved womin.
She den be alone behin hur plough. Lord, do hepp hur somhow.

8. DEM DARKIES

(A conversation between two young Union army soldiers.)

Wotta bout dem darkies?

Wotta bout wot?

Most caint even reed or rite.

Cood you reed or rite if you aint been teached?

Dem darkies smell bad too.

Wooden ya if youd be werkin all day, aint gittin no soap, and den be gittin a whippin wit a rope?

Wotta bout dat curly hair?

Yur hair too wood be lookin difrent if youd be comin frum whar dey comed frum.

Wotta bout dat darkie skin?

Yur skin wood be dark too if you be workin all day long in da hot sun.

Wot if dey all git guns?

Den dey cood be fighten fo da Union too, jest like we be doin. And den dey be savin dare youngins and jest bein free.

Wot if dey git freed?

Well, wood ya den be less free? Youd be okay, and I be okay too.

Wot if Lincoln free'm somtime?

I be hopin he will somday soon. Why do ya fear dem darkies so much?

Dem darkies aint like you and me.

> Well, no possum be like you and me. Wez all be difrent. Wot be happenin whence ya left home?

I dunno, I jest be leavin home to be joinin dis fedral army.

> And you had nun tryin to hunt ya down or to be killin ya? Dats becuz yur white'n free.

So, dey jest wonts to be free, like you and me?

> Dats right. Let'm be gittin a mule and som land, and jest be seein wot happens. You okay wit dat?

I still dunno.

> Spoze I be now knowin wots in yur troubled soul, wit its huge and hateful hole. Whence in battle, you be runnin whilst dem darkie soldiers will be soon dyin. Dey be brave, aint like you be.

> You be lazy, dem darkies ain't. Whence you be dead, I be hopin in Hell you be rottin. Yur jest a godly deceiver, whilst each Darkie I be knowin seemz a true believer.

> You caint no longer be my possum, dats true. I will be no longer defendin you. Whilst you be keepin on chidin dem darkies, I shalt not be agin abidin you.

9. OVER TIME

Twas once a civie enlistin. Den a recruit in trainin, to be soon enuff a soldier killin. Twas later a proud wounded vetran healin wit no future to be revealin.

Twas once too young to be afraid, and den too painfulee old to proudlee parade. Twas later not much respected; except jest by da survivin men of my brigade.

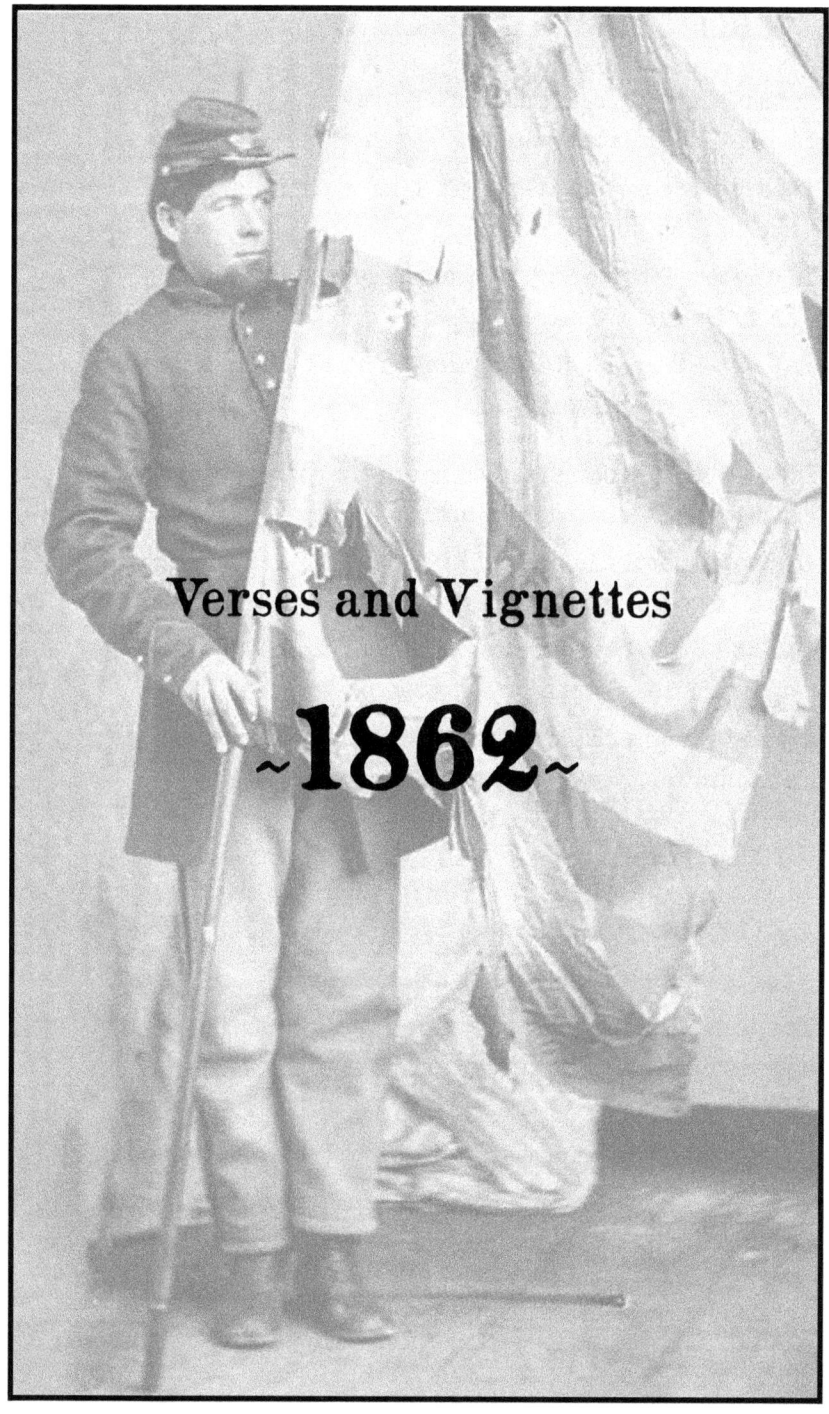

Verses and Vignettes
~1862~

10. BEEN BETTER

Tiz much awful cold, and I oft be wearin my
  betrothed-knitted sweater.
Twas much appreciated, but I be wishin
  she not be such a worrier.
In dis war, I be mor afraid to be badlee wounded
  or to be quite sicklee.
But now I must be stayin strong, and at times brave,
  and very much lucky.

Like othas, I wood ratter be havin my body whole,
  and bein safe in a futur home,
Dan to be rottin in som cold wooden coffin,
  headin to a hometown grave alone.
Whilst I still bein blessed in da confusion
  of meaninless battle, I hav been better.
I jest be hopin dat my betrothed will soon be
  stitchin up my war-torn sweater.

11. WAITIN' AND PRAYIN'

She be waitin and prayin. Derz not much else
  fur a lonelee married woman to do,
Den to be waitin fur som letters frum a husband,
  son or brotha to be replyin to.
She be prayin fur dare safe return,
  stead of receivin dat official army letter at hur door.
And bein fearful of readin da newspaper widits long list
  of deaths by da score.

Doze wives will be repairin dem uniforms,
  makin blankets, and fillin sandbags too.

Som be devoted women be workin in hospitals,
   heppin ar wounded boys in blue.

Dey be knowin dare men struggle to reunite dis Union
   and to be endin dis slavery sin.

And will do so widout complainin, doze stoic women
   ar waitin and prayin fur ar reunion.

12. NEW RECRUITS

Doz wide-eyed recruits and steely-eyed vetrans
   all be bivouacin togetter.

Dey be wearin dare Union blue wit spit-polished brass
   and buff-blacked leather.

Each nite, som recruits be foolishlee tradin
   godawful campfire stories,

Wit dare unrealistic visions of som futur
   ghostlee battlefield glories.

On a brisk autumn dawn, dey be marchin southward
   wit dare laden packs,

And be carryin dare shiny bayoneted-rifles
   and doz over-stuffed haversacks.

By dayz dusk, dem survivors be caked wit salty sweat
   and red Virginie mud,

Whilst many otha campfire comrades lay bullet-dead
   in pools of shared blood.

Nitelee, dem recruits be standin in e'er shorter lines
   waitin fur grits and stew,

Realizin dat many othas will be missin
   da mornins role call at next dayz' dew.

Somday dis relentless devastation be finally endin,
   if da blessed Lord wood be so willin.

Dey all be knowin dey caint be stopin dis
   relentless marchin and butcherin.

Az a Union army regular, my private's life
   waz oft demandin and ruff.
Twas wounded at Bull Run and den shot agin
   atop de cliffs of Ball's Bluff.
Da countless Reb rank volleys felled many of
   ar strongest and most brave.
Whenced dare cannons be stopin; many Blues be restin
   in a unmarked grave.

So far, I be one of da lucky ones who may once agin
   feel da heat of homestead hearth.
And I be hopin to be see my wife's freckled face,
   and to be feelin hur sweet warmth.
Afta Taps, I oft be recallin hur special laugh
   and da soft intimacy of ar recollected love.
While bein bad wounded, I be not ready fur peace
   in God's o'er-burdened heaven abuv.

13. COPPERHEADS AND HOOKERS

I jest be thinkin doze Copperheads wer dangerous poison snakes,
   And dat dem hookers wer jest som sad befallin fancy gals.
But I be knowin doze Copperheads ar connivin Reb conspeertors,
   Wit many livin in da shadows and sabotagin ar towns up North.

And doze hookers wer jest bein Gen. Hooker's camp-followers,
   But dey wer also wives, vivanders, sutlers, nurses, and so forth.
Doze camp-followers be cookin, launderin, and sewin,
   Jest to be makin da lives of dem brave soldiers a tad bit easyer.

Mong dem wer som dat be exploitin som hapless fedral soldiers,
  Like da grifter, de carpetbagger, or dat lonelee man-pleaser.
I jest be thinkin doze Copperheads wer dangerous poison snakes,
  And dat dem hookers wer jest som sad befallin fancy gals.

14. IRONCLADS CLASH

Dat Reb frigate *Merrimack* be limpin into Norfook
  afta hur Sumpter shellin.
Twas rebuilt by Gosport shipbuilders wit som iron coatin
  befor hur fateful renamin.
Tween dem rivers York and James, doze Peninsular battles
  wer commencin,
And dis newborn ironclad twas now emergin to be slowin
  da Union advancin.

De *Virginie*, once da *Merrimack*, begint hur history
  by shootin hur cannons well.
And soon doz Union warships, da *Cumberland, Congress*
  and *Minnesota*, all quick fell

Den, lika ghost outta de Chespeake mist,
  de fedral ironclad suddenlee be appearin.

Fur hours, da *Monitor* be tradin hur lethal cannon shots
  wit no victor be declarin.

Frum Fortress Monroe, one cood see da *Monitor's* shells
  wer bouncin off Virginie's deck.

But soon afta, da Rebel ironclad be shatterin da *Monitor's*
  pilothouse all to bludee heck.

Suddenlee, in a surprisin vasive maneuvre, da *Virginie*
  skilfulee be runnin hurself aground.

And at dusk, twas dislodged to be headin to
  a Tidewater dock, preparin fur anotha round.

Afta da damaged *Monitor's* witdru, Yorktown fell
  to Union cannon and soldier mini ball.

Bein outflanked, da Rebel navy den be surrenderin
  its *Virginie* and otha frigates all.

Not wantin *Virginie* to be a trophy, de Rebel navy
  be destroyin dat victorious ironclad.

Den da Chespeake Bay waz Union safe, and Richmond
  crumbled to dat Billy Yank lad.

15. THE UNFORGIVEN

Too soon, da youthful years of happiness wer fast furgotten.
Why do dat fedral army life havin to be so terrible rotten?

Why do we let doz Reb soldiers die wit dare intact dignity?
Dey be attackin us furst! So do dey deserve ainy lastin amitee?

He, who be lovin dis nation united, need not too soon furgive.
So, we must forcefulee win dis war if da Union iz to live

16. NIGHT PICKET

I be da new nite picket corporal. Alwayz bein
   silent, alert, and tense.
Why do I still be thinkin of my family farm's
   whitewashed peelin fence?
Dat patchy fence be circlin once vibrant,
   but now wiltin, bluebells.
And my betrothed do be patientlee waitin
   fur my promised church bells.

My scattered home thoughts ar ne'r to othas
   be in-public spoken.
So I be keepin nite vigilant, or tiz coffin-nails
   if I be tobac smokin.
My picket orders ar bein sent by hand-waved signals,
   so very secret.
Jest one mistake cain be resultin in bein da sharpshooter's
   next target.

Recentlee, dare waz a showy young picket private
   I ne'r reelee knew.
He waz less vigilant dan othas; and be talkin loud
   afta da evenin tattoo.
De nite befo de Antietam battle, dis private waz agin
   bein stupid slack.
And now hiz family, and bride-to-be, shall be wearin
   funeral black.

By dawn, all my nite pickets be stayin alive by bein
   silent, alert, and tense.
Dey all be knowin dat otha private did unwiselee die
   in dis ole forest dense.

Dat sharpshooter be makin him a trophy, and we ne'r agin
be hearin hiz laughin.

Fur me, I'd ratter be stayin alive, and be sharin my vows
at my hometown weddin.

17. VOLUNTEER'S DIARY

(A soldier recalls the loss of his friend's diary.)

> I be sayin my good-byes to my family and friends, and to my special gurl too. And now be puttin som thoughts inta sentences. I be decidin to keep a daily diary to be archivin my personal thoughts, and som of my futur infantry experiences. Twas den taken to da army recruitin office. And wit my personals, be marchin off to da nearby local train station. So now my new soldierin adventure be startin az a 90-day volunteer fightin to be savin dis shaky Union . . .

Day 1 - Friday, tiz hot. I now be usin my new quill and inkpot to be writin down my thoughts. Looks like I be needin som wood planks too fur a make-do desk. So wher to be startin?

I be both proud and anxious at da same time. I now be livin a strange new life. I be trainin hard and drillin well to becom a good soldier too. But furst, I must be gittin my Private's uniform, yankee blue.

Dis furst day iz finalee o'er. Thankfulee! I be totlee exhausted and sore. I be needin to be takin care of my blisters all. Soon I be hopin to be makin new friends. But tonite I be sleepin well until reveille's earlee mornin call. Morrow shood be much easier once I be gittin to know da solderin routines. But now tiz too soon to tell. Morrow, my Furst Sargent be talkin bout marchin south. Iz dare reelee dat big a need to be headin into Hell?

Day 2 - Saturday, tiz much cooler today. Better to be drillin in da mornin and to be ponderin my futur a bit later. Soon I be washin my clothes, shinin my cup'n cutleree, and polishin my boots. 88 mor days to go. Do dat madder rite now? I jest be gittin my new rifle. Tiz a bran new Springfield. Need to be knowin how to be takin it apart and puttin it back togetter, fast.

So wherz my book of Hardee drill? Need to be restin and lettin my sore body heal. Den I be walkin bout da camp tryin to be meetin som othas who cain cook az good az me.

>>>

Day 31 – Yestaday, shood hav been mor special. Doz days ar beginin to blur. Still 59 mo long days to go. Trainin iz gittin easier. I be gittin fit. We oft be hearin bout da frontline news and see dem Union trains full of da wounded goin by slow and headin back up north. Glad I still be gettin packages frum home and I be liken my new corncob pipe. Tiz nice to be missed. Time to be workin in da camp kitchen. Peelin som taters and learnin how to cook fur many othas. Gotta be goin soon.

>>>

Day 63 – 27 mor days to go. We be leevin dat trainin camp a lifetime ago. Twas furst in da rear-guard, and den later, be fightin som in da van. Twas a bit scary bein on da frontlines. Afta many of dem smaller skirmishes, we den got into a big one. I be recallin dat som of my new buddies be gittin blowed to kingdom com. One moment yur alive; and in da next, yur gone.

War iz terabull; but som words be makin it lika mild skufull. Like 'engagement' (notta weddin), 'encounter' (notta meetin), and 'campaign' (notta political activity). Tis awful! Dis war iz horrifyin, but doz words be tryin to make it sound heroic. It aint.

>>>

Day 80 – 10 days to go. By countin' em down, it be givin me som hope. At da same time, time be passin by too slow and too fast too. Tiz much confusin. You somtimes be sleepin in da day and be fightin at night. Ne'r ainy time to fullee plan; but som officers be startin to be listenin to my reasonin. I be seemin to hav a nack fur battle plannin. My advice iz somtimes bein sought. So I be writin my ideas togetter wit som supportin ideas. My fingers be crossin fur som mo good thinkin. Den maybeI can be stayin away frum doze deadly frontlines.

Day 81 - Tiz goin to be cooler today. At least tiz startin out dat way. I be headin home in 9 days; but how? Been months of bloodshed wit many mo soldier-friends now bein dead. Livin iz jest here and now. I be learnin to fight smarter, and whence to be skedattlin. And how to be gittin ready fur anotha day of woe. Yet, I be stayin focused.

My leadership in da van waz bein noticed agin. And yestaday, twaz promoted to corpral. Huzzah! Iz my futur in de army realy bein discussed serious? De 1st Sargt be wantin me to re-enlist fur 90 mo days. So am I ready to be advancin wittin da ranks of Blue? I be tellin him I be ponderin on it. But no. I be seein too much mizry and death. So wots an ole 90-dayer to do? Tiz simple, jest be stayin alive.

Day 82 - Wot will dis dewy day be bringin? In jest 8 mor days, do I be goin home by horse, by train, or by jest walk away frum all dis mess?

Da 1st Sargt jest be leavin my tent. I be tellin him no thanks cuz my fright waz real. I cood be makin som big mistakes, I did confess. If so, othas wood die cuz of me. He be sayin we all be havin fear, even him. And dat dis fear be makin him a better soldier. I waz told dat my men be listenin and followin my evry call. Ev'n so, I agin be sayin no thanks. Until I go, I be givin my men, my 1st Sargt and dis Fedral Union, my very all.

Later he be re-enterin my small tent to be tellin me som bad news. My two new units of men ar now in da 2nd wave. To be fillin up da Yankee gaps? I be knowin dat gaps be meanin too many Yanks got kilt. And so will my men. Death shall be comin mo faster morrow. By evenin, afta da battle, too many will n'er agin hear dem evenin Taps.

Day 83 - Da weather dint seems to mattar ainy mo. I now be facin 7 mor days of carnage befo I be runnin home or stealin a horse. Last night twaz preparin fur my 2nd wave duties. Be needin to be explainin it good to my soldier boys. My corpral's voice iz gettin mo sorelee. Soon we be musterin soon. Gotta be goin now. Dis battle aint awaitin fur no one, specialee me.

So glad dis bludee day iz o'er. Ar battle plan went awry agin. Too many of my boys be layin dead. We survivors be limpin slo back to camp. Doze officers be listenin to my ideas, but dey not be followin dem. It be makin me mad. Today, I be losin many a young lad.

Da sawbones be soon patchin up my wounds so I can be gittin ready fur da morrow's renewal of death. My spirit iz evenin damp.

Da 1st Sargt be stoppin by to see my wounds and be makin me a Sargt fur today's valor. My boys dint battle-cave. Doze dead ar da real heroes. He den be giftin me hiz own sergeant's sword. Wot an honor he be stowin on me. At sunrise, we now be in de deadly 1st wave. It be a harsh reward fur not gittin kilt today? Shood we be gittin ready fur anotha mass Union grave? You cain be seein dem grave-diggers gittin ready. Not good fur morale.

Day 84 - Wotta beautiful dawn, but tiz ne'er a good day to be dyin. Tiz too hot. Why do I keep countin down my days? Seems a bit triflin. Do I believe I cain be makin it till den? Take a deep breff. Be composed. I must be showin som bravery fur my boys. Yet, dey already be knowin how to be men. What do I be sayin to lead doze men? We be knowin dat 'at all costs' be meanin we all be bullet fodder. Ar we agin to be da price fur a righteous cost sublime? Yep, I still do be believin dat dis Union iz worth dyin fur. Da fedral mission iz mighty righteous and good. We jest be needin to be reminded mo bout dat frum time to time.

I be thinkin, I may ne'r be seein my dirt-floor tent agin? How sad iz dat? Frum dawn till dusk, I be knowin my men will be fightin widout too much fear. All fur now. Gotta go.

Too soon combat came hand-to-hand violent; but som of us do be survivin. Too tired to be thinking of what be happenin today. But befor I cood be fallin asleep, da 1st Sargt came a callin agin. I be so tired of hiz ev'r changin plans. No rest, we agin ar in da furst wave. I be now tryin to a bit revive. I be needin som sleep.

Day 85 - Da rain iz much welcomed. A blessed relief. Jest 5 mo days to be carryin my wounds home, both seen and unseen. Bein now a new Sargt, I be havin many mo lads to lead. Wit mo lads be meanin dat mo parents, I may be soon writin dem sad news. Today, will we all be rebel-sacrificed to a fate unforeseen? I be blamin not da 1st Sargt fur dis battle plan. Tiz doz glory seekin officers who be messin up agin and agin. Yes, dare mistakes mean mo Yanks will die, and perhaps da battle lost. Perhaps I shood be re-enlistin. Not fur me but fur my men. I believe I kin be savin mo of dem. I do not lie.

Jest be returnin frum my 1st Sargt's tent. I be re-enlistin! He den surprizinly be orderin me and my men back to da rear. We shall soon be quick-marchin by 8s. So wots really goin on? An extra day of livin? Such a burden relieved. I now be gittin som rest and washin' som cloths, and doin som reflectin and writin home. I also be takin a big sigh of relief. At least my tater-peelin and picketin daze ar o'er.

Day 86 - Tiz early mornin, and now I be havin only 4, and 90, mor days to go. Tiz barely daylight, but cain now hear dem rebel cannons roarin in da distance. How faraway do dey be? Dey seem to be gittin louder and louder. I be havin no fears. Need to finish dat letter home to let my family know of my decision to be re-enlistin. Dis will surely bring'em tears. My mothar and fathar shall be much disappointed and be much distressed. But fur now, I be hopin to save my many lads frum dare parents' woe. Wots dat? Splosions all round! Ar we unda a Reb attack?

Dat new sargent be droppin hiz quill and spillin hiz inkpot. He be needing to rally hiz men, and be off runnin into da chaos.

Shortlee afta dis shockin Rebel attack began, da 1st Sargt be gallopin fast to da new Sargt's tent. Twas totalee obliterated. All blowed apart. Ev'rythin twas splintered and scattered. No Sargt to be found. Must go, da Union counter sally shall soon be startin.

>>>

Day 90 – *Afta finalee repellin de Rebel's sneak attack, da 1st Sargt do solemnly be packin da missin new Sargt's gear. He be findin som torn family photos, burnt letters frum home, a corncob pipe, and a half-written letter. But wherz hiz diary dear? Not here hidin in da carnage.*

Perhaps, somone will be findin it later. Soon da 1st Sargt be writin da new sargt's family on how dare shy quiet lad had become a good leader wit too much bravery. Hiz men wood be agreein.

When dat battle ended, da new Sargt's body waz found by hiz loyal comrades, along wit hiz bludee ne'r used sword. But no diary to be found. Dey den be placin a wooden cross abuv da sergeant's grave inscribin hiz bravery in da Union's newlee dug burial site. Dey all be knowin de army's mission be remainin da same: to be savin da Union and to be endin dat terribel sin of slavin.

In time, dat new Sargt's family wood be receivin a Lincoln letter appreciatin dare son's sacred sacrifice, wit da president's deepest sympathy. Dat 1st Sargent wood be later visitin hiz parents and be deliverin dare son's new sword, now clean. Sadlee no diary waz found.

18. SCAVENGER

(A soldier finds a personal item.)

Afta each fierce and bludee fight,
  many survivors be havin lost som sacred coutrements.
Wit uniforms tattered, dey be tryin to find ainy items lost,
  like dare kepis, boots, haversacks, buttons or bayonets.

Tiz official army policy fur each soldier Blue,
  to be returnin dare battle-worn uniforms fullee intact.
If not, doze survivors shall be havin dare pay much deducted
  fur all dare damaged or missin items. A woeful fact.

Each mornin, som survivors of da yestadays' slaughter,
  will befo da muster be gatherin to battleground explore.
At furst, I be feelin guilty; but my scavengin did stop da army
  frum reducin my monthly wage. Both wer acts to abhor.

Ar fallen heroes be no longer needin doze soldierin
  coutrements dat once agin can still be much re-used.
I be havin e mixed feelins bout my battlefield scavengin,
  and I ne'r be desecratin da fallen's honor. Non wer abused.

Som be needin dem extra needles and threads fur dare
  housewifery kits to do som portant uniform sewin and mendin.
And I be findin mo of dem kit gubbins dey always be needin,
  so I be preparin dem fur my sellin or tradin.

Befo I be thinkin dat scavengin twas truly evil,
  but twas all too handy fur me, frum one time or anotha.
Whilst inspectin doz fallen Blue, I oft be findin personal items,
  to be sent later to a grievin father or mother.

Perhaps, I too will be found battle dead. Den, az a slain brotha,
  I still be heppin doz brothas be finishin dare Union mission.
Twood be my last gift to be savin my comrades frum doze pay deductions,
  jest cuz som of dare dispensible coutrements be battle missin.

Tiz my last hope dat if ainy of my personal items ar to be found,
  dey wood den be in time sent homeward bound.
Alas, I be enlistin to fight doze traitorous back-stabbin Rebs,
  not to be scavengin Union bodies on doze battlegrounds found.

Afta my last afta-battle savengin, I be feelin not so grand,
  I be findin da body of my closest friend wit a diary in hiz hand.
Hiz last entry waz a plea to be sendin ainy personals to hiz family,
  and I will do so, afta cleanin hiz blood-soaked diary.

We wer once tent partners. Twaz proud of him, no denial.
  I be now honored to be speakin at da new Sargt's burial.
I be later hand-deliverin hiz diary, and personals, a corncob
  pipe, and wit da gift of his Furst Sargt's sword.
And I do be hopin he be livin in heaven az hiz final reward.

19. YURS, BUT NOT OURS

Army chaplains wood oft be forgivin dare own army's atrocities,
  whilst ne'r forgivin doz of da enemy. Such pious hypocrisies.

Army officers wood oft be forgivin a wayward soldier's doin wrong,
  but ne'r be forgivin a worthy soldier fur jest bein right all along.

20. KING COTTON

If King Cotton reigns, da South shall be punishin
  its African property wit doz whips and chains.
And if da Union loses dis war, dat slavery remains,
  den doz slave owners will n'er giv up doz ill-gotten gains.

Da Confedrit's Constitution now be legalizin dis human abusage,
  and be providin a safe harbor to dem ships of bondage.
Tiz now da time to be endin dis sad, barbaric, and inhuman carnage,
  by totalee winnin dis bludee war. Tiz Lincoln's pledge.

21. STARS OR BARS?

Da Confedricy be wavin its 'Stars and Bars' brazenlee,
  as bein proud of its 2nd war fur independency.
Dareby, unda it, be creatin a new God-fearin nation,
  dat believes in States' Rights and subjugation.

Da Union be seein dis Reb flag az proof of treason.
  and goin to be destroyin dis fedral union.
Dis Dixieland be wantin da slave-rich men to be equals all,
  whilst all women and darkies be havin no rights at all.

Da Union be seein 'Old Glory' az a proud proclamation,
  of its fairness, equality and emancipation.
By bludee Fedral mandate to be keepin da Union whole,
  can be ensurin equal rights in evry State. Dats da goal.

Da Rebs be seein da Union flag az a God-less boastin,
  and be feedin its greedy fedral intrusion and ov'r reachin.
Dis reunited Union wood be diminishin and destroyin,
  dat southern way of legalizin da whitemans ov'rseerin.

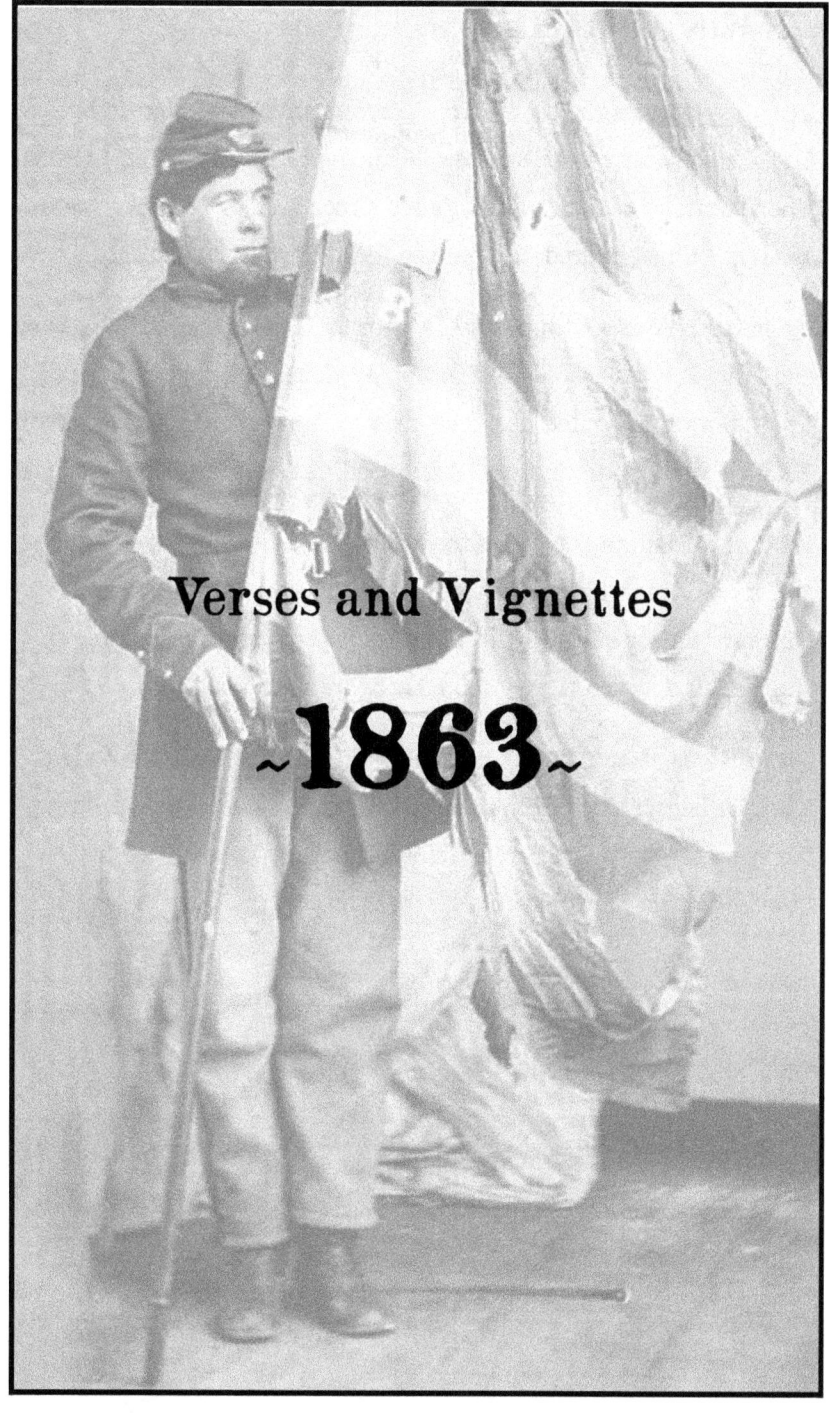

Verses and Vignettes

~1863~

22. WINTER BATTLE

I caint wait to agin be feelin my hometown's soft summer breeze.
But furst, we must be winter camp marchin at sunset freeze.
I be wearin my stiff frosted, faded frockcoat to fire-glow warm.
Awaitin to be ordered to foe-man flank in wintery storm.

By 4s, we be quick-steppin to da nearby creek's once-frozen ford,
And into icy waters we be sloggin, az doze hot cannons roared.
My high spirits cooled az we be crossin into dat now-slushy creek.
Glad my kepi be blockin da harsh wind dat be piercin each cheek.

Thru a wooded gap, I be seein dis battle haz fiercelee begun.
And my muddied boots, once ford-wet, be now solid frozen.
I be prayin dis midnight skirmish will end befor daylite sun.
Cuz o'ernite, my cold and achy limbs ar agin gone numb.

Gittin to da frontlines, I be hearin da bullets whistlin o'erhead.
I can be hearin doze dyin soldiers moanin wit dare bodies shred.
Perhaps to jest snow-drift die, wood not be so terrible bad.
But onward go I into dis bludee battle, a scared and frigid lad.

23. GLORY OR DEATH

Dare wer two great armys wit a millyon feet,
  to be clashin wherev'r glory and death shall meet.
We be patientlee waitin fur da evenin Taps and drum.
  I be knowin dat peace shall ventualee com.

We once be prayin fur da victorz gloryus crown,
  only to be slaughtered wit lil or no renown.
Shall we die wit som patriotic lust,
  and be revered by doze livin abuv da dust?

Oft times, dare be no escapin dis deadlee mayhem,
  only to be felled by da enemy's lethal bedlam.
Ar fightin spirit wont quietlee yield,
  we be not ready to die in coffined field.

Too many shall be joinin dat democracy of da dead,
  leavin dare families befo dey bein church wed.
Lord, pleze be allowin dez dead frum evry proud State,
  to be peacefulee enterin Saint Peter's Gate.

Whence dis uncivil war be endin, jest one flag shall fly.
  Whilst it be 'Old Glory' or da 'Bars' be wavin in de sky?
Many soldiers at Gettysburg, and otha places, did bravelee fall.
  Lord, do be rememberin doze lads wer Americans all.

We be impatientlee waitin fur evenin Taps to forev'r cease,
  az we be solemnlee prayin fur a General-made peace.
Yep, dare wer two great armys wit a millyon feet,
  to be clashin wherev'r glory and death shall meet.

24. GETTYSBURG REVISITED

Cuz da Union army be lackin som aggressive fight,
   Bobby Lee be testin its fedral resolve and might.
Da Rebs wer repulsed on flank left and on flank right.
   Den Gen Lee wood be plannin all thru da nite.

Hiz strategy waz simple, and hiz actions to be bold.
   But Pickets men wer heaven-bound, history soon told.
Az Pickets advancin' files wer slawturd by Meades guns,
   Doz green fields wer soon coated by dead southern sons.

Clashin bayonet to bayonet stood Johnny Reb and Billy Yank,
   and death cam too quicklee, rank afta rank afta rank.
De moanin of doze dyin graybacks be replacin dare once-proud yells,
   to soon be followed by da sobbin of plenty Dixie belles.

Neath dat Lincoln-consecrated, now silent, battlefield,
   ar many boys dis hallowed ground shall ne'r yield.
Dis bloodthirsty rebellion be dragin on fur mor agonizin years.
   Nothin cain be stopin dis killin, not ev'n doz endless tears.

25. DRUMMERS, SIGNALLERS, AND BUGLERS

In da noise, smoke, and chaos of battle,
  how do dem officers be givin dare portant orders?
Dey be usin da talents of dem young drummer boys,
  well-trained signallers and skilful buglers.

Doze drummer boys be beatin out dare officers messages,
  to dem embattled field commanders.
Doze signalers be silentlee wavin dare critical orders,
  to dem fightin frontline officers.
And doze buglers be powerfulee soundin out dare commands,
  to dem newly re-positioned van soldiers.

So effective wer dey, dat doze enemy sharpshooters
  wood be tryin to kill'em off double-quicklee.
But de officers soon be findin dey wer easy replaced,
  by som otha patriots dat be volunteerin promptlee.

26. ELEPHANTS
(Soldiers often called large-scale battles Elephants.)

Befo da Elephant, we be volunteerin fur battles gloryus.
   No time fur bein sorry.
Wit newlee blackened haversacks and whitened gaiter spats,
   We be marchin stout-heartedlee in frockcoats and Hardie hats.
We be talkin of ar futurs and be braggin bout captured
   booty wit som story.
We oft be cleanin ar Springfields and be polishin ar cups of tin.
   And be drillin in ar woollen trousers and shirts of muslin.
Befo da Elephant, we be volunteerin fur a battle's glory.
   No time fur ainy worry.

Afta da Elephant, derz no mor glorious morrows.
   No time fur ainy sorrow.
Wit empty haversacks, and wit ar briar-ripped trousers
   and tattered spats,
We be stumblin on wit bullet-torn frock coats
   and mud-smeared hive-hats.
We be talkin no mor of da futur, wit no treasures found,
   and no stories bout de morrow.
Wit rustin battle-warm Springfields and ar crushed cups of
   coffee-stained tin,
We be gittin no thread to needle-sew uniforms or soap to
   be washin dirty muslin.
Afta da Elephant, derz no need fur battles gloryus,
   and too much time fur sorrow.

27. AFTERMATH

Afta da violent combat comed to a bludee end,
  evry soldier be nitelee searchin fur a missin friend.
The fallen wer gathered az dare bodies be startin to stiffin,
  and da smell of doz dead be steepin de air we be whiffin.
Afta doze dead warriors wer stilt-stacked like woodland lumber,
  dey be havin no mor fear, only startin dare eternal slumber.

We survivors be havin uniforms once-covered wit sash and fringe,
  ar now covered in dryin blood and gun-powdered singe.
Befor, we be havin fearless eyes, but now dare tired and bloodshot,
  and we now still be dreadin dat cannon roar and grapeshot.
Doz not wounded wood to be quick-stockin dare mini-ball tins,
  and be tryin to forgit da litnee of doze past battlefield sins.

Doze man-boys livin finalee earned dare well-deserved rest,
  and dem unfortunates be takin dare leave frum futur test.
Dem officers to be drinkin doze whisky stocks now liberated,
  whilst de volunteers be chewin tobac in barren orchards picketed.
Morrow, dare be no retreatin. We win de battle, or to die in defeat.
  Da true aftamath of war iz whence victory tiz totlee complete.

28. MISSING

Did hiz blud soak into dat muddy battlefield today?
  Wher, o'er time, will doze wildflowers agin be growin?
Did my good ole friend be dyin in peace or in pain?
  Did hiz death e'er matter to you? I'll ne'r be knowin.

I oft be hearin dat hiz fightin spirit waz passionate,
   and dat he waz oft very bold and brave.
But hiz body waz not yet found.
   Do he be layin in som unseen grave?
Forevr a mistery? Did he die fur naught? I be hopin not.
   Fur me, he shall ne'r be forsakin or furgotten.
Som be sayin he battle-cracked and den deserted.
   Wit no body be found, tiz somthin be smellin rotten?
Wich he be, dead-missin or alive-missin?
   Back home dey awl be soon a wonderin.
Somday will he be walkin thru da front door?
   Or be he a deserter disappearin forevr mor?

29. FRIENDSHIP

Hiz name waz Caleb, and hiz story be short and very sad.
Caleb's father died of som pox whence he waz jest a yung lad.
He be heppin hiz mother and hiz sisters work da farmstead clay.
Den, he be joinin da army to earn som monthlee pay.

Caleb dint join de army to be fightin doz secesh betrayers.
He joined to be payin off doze family farm debt collectors.
In hiz furst battle, Caleb panicked and he be takin flight.
But waz caught by hiz blue brothas befo da day twas nite.

Dat evenin, a tribunal be findin him guilty of desertion.
By next mornin, an army chaplain be grantin som absolution.
At noon, Caleb waz sayin hiz last words,
   whence de officer yelt wit ire.
Loud and clear, Billy be hearin da orders.
   Reddy...Aim...(Who do dat earlee fire?)

Private Caleb's friend Josh waz on dat firin squad.
  He be knowin him well. Twaz a boyhood friend.
Corporal Josh waz a shur-shot farmer. So he be makin sur
  dat Billy be havin a quick and painless end.
So whence Caleb be seein him, he be givin Josh a nod.
  Twas o-k to be sendin him to hiz God.
Dat officer twas much mad at Josh. He soon be disciplined,
  but Josh twas still a proud sod.
He now be sendin home the personals of hiz friend,
  and later be lyin bout Caleb bein brave.
And he shall ne'r be revealin Calebs unmeant cowardice
  awl da way to hiz own grave.

30. MUSIC AT 100 PACES

...Twas a mild evenin wit a slight wind breezin whence Isak be startin hiz nitelee picket duty. Soon, he be hearin som Reb fiddle music frum cross dis now sleepy battlefield. Twas it Stephen Foster's 'Swanee Ribber'? Suddenlee, da music be stopin.

Hey Yank, Billy Yank. You out thar?

> **Yep, Reb. Wot you want, Johnny?**

Got time fur som music? We needa break frum whippin yur bluebelly ass today.

> **Wer not like yuz yella dogs always be runnin away. Indeed, sounds good. You go furst.**

...Den frum cross da frontline van, Isak cood be hearin som ole southern melodies. To hiz surprize, twas quite calmin...

Yank, ya got ainy good drummers or fiddlers o'er ther? Or did we kill all dem mudsills?

> **Nah, you muggins caint shoot true. I reckon we still do. Yep, we got som live ones!**

...Durin da back-and-forth tween da rival pickets, som Union musicians be gadderin. Afta a short while, som northern tunes wer bein played wit sturin passion. Dem Rebel soldiers respectfulee be listenin to da 'Battle Hymn,' bein followed by da 'Battle Cry'...

Hey Billy, not bad. Try to be keepin doz boys frum gettin shot dead.

...Frum cross da moonlit meadow, n'er to be outshined, came a chorus of 'Southern Soldiers' bein followed by 'Dixie.' Agin twas a strange hush fell mong doze combatants. Twas a respectful atmosphere bein created?...

> Well done, Johnny. You be havin ainy Irish boys o're ther? If dare still breathin, lets be hearin 'em.

...But furst, da Union musicians started playin 'Saint Patrick's Day.' Whence done, da Confederate musicians be respondin wit dare 'Confedrit Irish Brigade.' Huzzahs cood be heard frum both sides of dat no-man's land...

Billy, ya ready fur som good ole marchin music?

> Yep. We be goin furst if dats okay wit you.

...Doze Union musicians be playin 'Tramp, Tramp' and 'Gary Owen'—and da Confedrit musicians be replyin wit dare 'Bonnie Blue Flag' and da 'Yellow Rose.' Both sides wer truly enjoyin dis musical competition. Isak be enjoyin doze Reb fiddlers and banjo players...

...In da silent times, Isak oft thought bout dis war. Ar we Yanks fightin to be preservin da Union or fur doze big and greedy northern companies? Ar we jest be dare cannon fodder? Ar doze Rebs really fightin fur mor State's Rights or jest be appeasin dem slavin plantation owners? It be seemin like all us soldier boys ar jest pawns in dis savage chessboard war tween da rich. Evry day dis war be goin on, dey be only ones benefitin. Da music be startin agin?...

> Hey Johnny, we gotta stop. Ar officers be thinkin wer gittin too friendlee wit yawl. Lets do jest one mo song. Hey, wot ev'r be happenin to yur tenor? Such a handsom voice.

Well Yank, yawl shot'em dead two days ago. We be missin him too. Twas a good ole boy.

...All went quiet fur a moment. Den, one Union baritone soloist be softlee singin 'Weeping, Sad and Lonely' and dis be bringin tears to ev'n da most grizzled vetrans in Blue. Followin som silence, a soothin southern voice be commencin to sing 'Lorena.' And dis song too be havin a simlar effect on doze butternut-clad combatants. Now silence...

Sleep well, Billy. Yur gonna need it.

Goodnite, Johnny. You be ready. We be comin afta ya next sunrise.

...Den a wonderful surprise be occurrin. A lone voice be startin to sing 'Jeanie' and som choruses den beginned to be harmonizin frum evry direction. And ventualee, once da midnight moon silentlee be slippin behine som clouds, all de soldiers be needin to get som sleep fur morrows bedlam. Perhaps it be dare last nite of bein alive. Taps waz played. All Yanks now be sleepin, except fur Isak and hiz fellar picketers who wer still on de nite watch duty.

...And afta da next mornins reveille, de bludee mayhem began once agin, wit brothars killin brothars.

31. BUSHWACKER

My glory-driven officer waz a bully dat be buyin hiz title long befo.
Dat officer be cruelee leadin us into battle cauzin deaths by da score.

So I be plannin to git som revenge by schemin a unexpected plot.
And whence da timin iz good, I be takin dat shameless killin shot.

32. HEARTBROKEN

Why not me Lord?
Why not me!
Aint I ben faithful enuff fur Thee?

I wood die and be killin fur you and ar liberty.
But you be takin hur away frum me.

Hur sad pox death not be makin us free.
I now be havin no wife and no motha fur my chilins, three.

Why you be takin hur Lord? Iz dat my price fur liberty?
I be not fightin fur you, but jist fur my chilins and me.

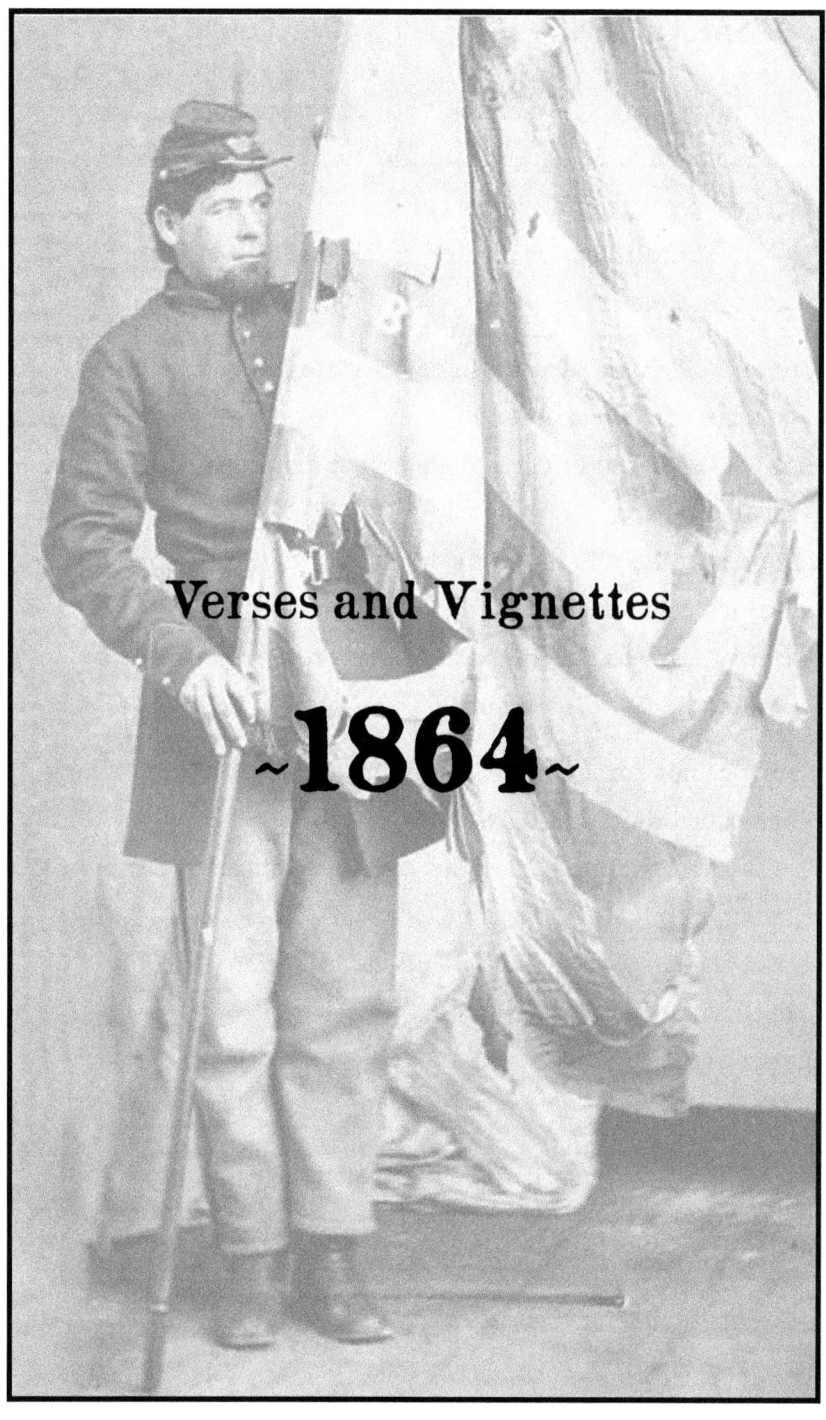

Verses and Vignettes

~1864~

33. SARAH JANE

Tiz ben two long years since James be army-enlistin. Bravo!
Miss Sarah Jane be expectin hiz letters each week. Not so.
Dare wer plenty good reasons fur Jimmy's chronic postal delayin.
Twas hiz battlin or drillin, or marchin or panickin,
  or be jest worrin.

Jimmy be fightin hard tryin to preserve dat shaky Union.
  No shame ther.
But Sarah be wishin fur a much sooner reunion and be needin
  som lovin care.
Like most places in da North, whilst all dem poor boys
  wer off rebel fightin,
Dem rich boys be stayin' home and be preyin upon doze
  boy-less ladies distressin.

Sarah be not forgetin hur Jimmy; but she be thrivin on hur
  new-found attenshun.
She be goin new-found places and seein new things wit hur new beau;
  but in hur letters, she dint ev'r mention.
Sarah still be writin Jimmy. But she be feelin guilty;
  but not quite guilty enuff.
Ders no good time to be tellin Jimmy da truth.
  Wooden dat be to so unkindlee ruff?

Sarah Jane be strugglin. She dint know when or how
  to be writin him bout hur bad news.
In hiz few letters, Jimmy be darin not to share hiz stories.
  Too gruesom to infuse.

Dis young lady need not be knowin da tragic facts of war
  and da daylee death he be facin.
But he shood hav been tryin mor. Hiz excuse waz
  to be protectin hiz Sarah, God-willin.

Miss Sarah be sendin dat awful letter dat no soldier
  be needin befo ainy battle dour.
But in dat terrible letter, she be shamefulee enclosin
  a Forget-Me-Not flower.
Dare relationship iz o'er. She be survivin, but he now
  be needin a new consequence.
Sarah Jane be marryin dat predator, but James be hopin
  fur a lass wit bedder sense.

34. BLUE DOGS

Army dogs be playin a portant Union miltary role,
  specialee durin dis tragic conflict immoral.
Som dogs be servin az prison camp guards,
  or to be much improvin dare soldier morale.

Othas be conveyin secret messages cross da frontlines,
  and be carryin bandages and medicines to da medics.
Som be savin wounded soldiers like dem Clara Barton nurses,
  and be foragin fur food, water and otha war-needed basics.

Othas, like da famous Dog Jack, be earnin som bravery medals,
  fur bein fearless like som of dare fellow man warriors.
And if dey be somtimes captured by som secech soldiers,
  der wer oft bein swapped fur som Rebel prizners.

35. HOME GUARD

Da Dixie Home Guard will be fightin to protect and defy,
  defend and die widout bein afraid.
Will de Confedritcee still stand, to be savin its slavry
  wit bravry, and at wot price paid?
Will dem Rebs be soundlee defeatin doz Yankee boys wit dare
  rezilence and tanacety?
Can da South build its new confederation
  of God-fearin Americans, ev'n mor perfectly?

Dey be fightin fur a successful secession, and widout ainy pay.
Doz Yankees be not takin daree beloved southern homeland away.
Dey radder die in Dixie dan to live in a godless country.

Dey be fightin wit great pride, and widout much munition.
Dey be forcefulee impedin da North's arrogant aggression.
Dey radder be hanged in public dan live in a northern Republic.

Dey be fightin wit great hope, and widout much food.
dey be protectin ar farms frum doze fedrals crude.
Dey radder be shot defendin' Georgia glory dan fur dat 'Ole Glory.'

Dey be fightin fur a Dixie future, and widout proper shoes.
Dey be makin dem wish dey ne'r wore doze Union blues.
Dey be Tennessean tuff till dey be havin pain enuff.

Dey be fightin fur a virtue true, and widout much recognition.
Dey be liberatin ar homeland frum dat Yankee ambition.
Dey be bringin Mississippian might to dis ne'r-endin fight.

Dey be fightin wit great zeal, and widout ainy Northern wealth.
Dey shall soon be findin dis Dixieland iz bad fur Yankee health.
Dey be Virginie valiant till Billy's brivouacs ar vacant.

Dey be fightin wit ar young and old, and widout ar Rebel men.
Dey be protectin ar birthright in each hollow and green glen.
Dey be Bama brave all da way to ar eternal Dixie grave.

Dey be fightin wit great chivalry, and widout ainy cavalry.
Dey be savin future generations ar pro-slavery dowry.
Dey be Arkansas ruff pushin dem Yanks o'er ev'ry bluff.

Dey be fightin longside family and friends, and widout ainy darkies.
Dey be restorin ar plantation life frum da Plains to da Keys.
Dey be usin som ole Texan tricks and git in ar bludee licks.

Dey be fightin longside ar vetran greybeards, and widout remorse.
Dey be takin on doze fedral trespassers, ten times ar force.
Dey be usin som Lou'siana luck till dare deep in bayou muck.

Dey be fightin longside ar scrappy remnants, and widout repentance.
Dey be stridentlee strugglin to win ar secund war fur independence.
Dey be Carolina cagey usin ar Rebel yellin and battlin crazy.

Dey be fightin longside ar farmers, and wit a battle plan.
Dey be ar still much better dan ainy New Englander man.
Der be no neutral Kentucky in ar new land of Dixie.

Dey be fightin wit ole rusty pistols and widout carbines or sabres.
Dey be savin awl southern states fur future plantation labors.
Az a nation, not yet grown, dey put Yanks in graves unknown.

We be fightin now wit blind courage, and widout much fear.
Dey be keepin on battlin fur dat Confederacy dey did so revere.
Even wit less boon dan bane, ar southern spirit shall ne'r wane.

Dat Dixie Home Guard did fight, dey protected and defied, defended and died.
But de Union still stands wid its bludee historiklee price bein scribed.

36. SKEDADDLE

Damn, jest anotha Union battle undulee lost,
   wit mor Billy Yanks bein da deadlee cost.
Given Yankee indecision and delay,
   doz VMI cadets gallantlee saved de day.

Doz cadets be joinin de tirin Reb militia brave,
   causin da Union flanks to woeflee cave.
Bein tacticlee out-maneuvred by Breckenridge,
   Sigel jest be escapin by da narrow bridge.

De Union army, bogged down in Virginie mud,
   twas lucky not to be loozin ev'nmor blood.
Damn, jest anotha Union battle undulee lost,
   wit mor Billy Yanks bein da deadlee cost.

37. WOMEN FOLK

Dey wur not tuff, but wur tuff enuff.
Dey bore life's yoke. dare ar womenfolk.
Dey be prunin da vine wit dignity divine,
And dey be tendin da cattle fur doz in battle.

Dey be workin in da heat whilst scythin da wheet.
Dey be catchin death's cold az dey be repairin shawls old.
Dey alwayz be havin da grace to be showin proud face,
And dey be sewin hope's quilt widout feelin much guilt.

Dey be prayin not fur a few, but all wearin da Gray or Blue.
Dey be feelin da nation's pain fur all doz menfolk slain.
Dey be fightin famine az dare men be fightin doz vermin,
And dey be provin dare worth wit lil hapiness or mirth.

Dey be writin to husbands and sons dat toted da guns.
Dey be havin much remorse fur each riderless horse.
Dey wur not tuff, but wur tuff enuff.
And dey bore life's yoke. Dey be ar womenfolk.

38. WILLOWS

A Bama widow woman had jest buried hur long-lovin husband,
  Jest befor dem Yanks be invadin dare barren farmstead land.
She be prayin dailee fur hur three courageous sons,
  Who now be unda a relentless siege by Union guns.

Da widow woman be lonelee ploughin hur unproductive fields.
  And not be expectin ainy bountiful blessins, jest scant yields.
In hur once-cozy farm, bein protected by damp hallows
  and tree-sheltered hills,
She be dreamin of hur son-hugs wit som homecomin thrills.

I, Soldier

Da widow woman oft be dressin up to be visitin
  hur husband's nearby grave.
And neath som tall willows iz a lone headstone
  wher hur wildflowers freelee wave.
Whence hur sons be returnin frum dis grim war,
  dey wood truly be farm-admirin.
Since dey be knowin how hard dis farmwork
  do be requirin.

Da widow woman be hearin dat many local boys
  had jest got kilt. Such tragic news.
In fact, each local son did fight bravelee;
  but all had perished, bein kilt by da Blues.
Soon doze tall willows will be providin a peaceful place
  wit its ev'rlastin shade,
Wher all de farmstead's patriotic menfolk shall soon be layed.
  Plans to be made.

Da widow woman iz now left alone
  wit hur sapped farm and wasted pride.
Twas dis Confedritcee be havin a just cause?
  Since fur it, awl hur menfolk had died.
She ne'r let anyone know how she be daylee cryin
  and nightlee weepin. Hur pain waz deep.
She be continuin hur chores; but privitlee,
  hur heart be longin fur God's eternal sleep.

Da widow woman be havin lil to sell,
  derz no slaves or farm animals to worry bout.
How to live widout hur ardent husband and lovin boys?
Twas dare ainy doubt?

Wher iz it? Tiz here somwher. Finelee, da widow
  be findin hur husband's carvin knife.
And widout delay, she be stridin to da willows;
  and by hiz headstone, be endin hur life.

> *... And who be now be placin dem wildflowers on doze graves?
> Or do dey awl jest forgottin?*

39. TOUGH DECISIONS

To give or to take? To save or to kill?
  Wot be my wartime options? Or tiz it jest God's Will?
To be givin ar imperfect Union anotha chance to exist,
  We must be denyin da Confedrit's secession wit Yankee fist.

To be savin ar Union's democratic liberty fur all,
  Must we be killin dat rebel spirit of ar southern brothas all?
So, to give, we must take; and to save, we must kill?
  God shall not be pickin a side. So it be jest ar Will.

40. NO LONGER

I caint be hearin doz cannons today, and dey ain't dat far away.
But I do be clearlee hearin da buzzin of a closeby bee.
And cain be smellin da dyin fruit on a nearby tree.
I be knowin I soon be dead, and no longer be havin tears to shed.

Many be purposelee dyin today, and be hopin fur peace wit Thee.
I no longer be hearin dat busy bee or be smellin dat fruity tree.
So here I be dyin alone, hopin to pass on wit som quiet dignity.
And az my home thoughts be driftin away, I be askin fur no pity.

41. DICE AND BEER

I caint clearlee be rememberin doz homespun yarns,
   bout dem gabled houses wit dare wooden barns.
And caint be forgettin da agonizin swamp fever death,
   of my soldier friend's last whimperin breath.
Tis still hard to be rememberin years past cleerlee,
   one's own family values, no longer held dearlee.
We be farmer-soldiers jest hopin to survive,
   wit som new wooden dice and icy cold beer.

I caint clearlee be rememberin drivin dat city-street buggy,
   on doze mornins, spring-dewy or summer-muggy.
And caint trulee be forgettin bout dem burnt-out family farms,
   wit doze vast fields of bodiless legs and arms.
Tiz still hard to be blankin out all dat daylee panic and fear,
   whist havin doze nitelee terrors. Tiz all so unclear.
We be city-soldiers jest hopin to survive,
   wit som used wooden dice and a lukewarm beer.

I caint clearlee be rememberin da sharin doz lil white lies,
   wit dat special girl, sharin hur tea and tastee fruit pies.
And caint be forgettin bout doz marchin blisters raw,
   or dat gritty grindin of da surgeon's bludee blunt saw.
Tiz still hard to be rememberin doz ole memories once clear,
   of all my boyhood pranks wit my friends livin near.
We be citizen-soldiers jest barelee survivin,
   wit som well-worn dice and ar last warm beer.

I caint clearlee be rememberin hur frilly dress of lace,
   nor even hur much freckled-covered smilin face.
And caint be forgettin doz disembowelled, ignoble foes,
   nor my own ne'r endin battlefield troubles and woes.
Tis still hard to be avoidin doz ever-present nitemares,
   az my God-willin and happy homecomin nears.
I now be a wounded vetran livin widout ainy dice or cheers,
   and be tryin to kill my pain wit opium and too many beers.

42. CLARA'S ANGELS
(A recovered wounded soldier remembers.)

Az doze boys be layin on da battlefield wounded,
   how can I be preventin dare needless dyin?
I be one of dem dedicated Barton-trained nurses
   tryin to delay destinyz daylee fateful preparin.

Wit doze othas devoted and tired frontline angels,
   we be heppin wore-out doctors be savin dem lucky ones.
We be disinfectin all dare medical tools and beds,
   and be softlee washin doz wounded fathas and sons.

Afta doze whiskey-drinkin doctors be life-or-death decidin,
  who will be havin dare damaged limbs severed.
We be nurses dat vigruslee be scrubin all dem bloodied tables,
  befo and afta da cuttin and sawin haz occurred.

Afta da surgery, doze brave soldiers, dat still bein alive,
  can oft painfulee still feel dare absent limbs throbin.
And do dem saintly nurses e'er be git used to all doze lads
  havin dare nitelee terrors and dare daylee screamin?

Who can be handlin teribull war daylee wit awl its dyin?
  fur doze frontline angels tiz a necessary must.
Dey be knowin wich families shall soon be weepin.
  and dey too weep; but doze nurses be stayin robust.

May God bless all doze frontline angels fur all dey be doin,
  by heppin doze boys be hopefulee recoverin well.
Dey too be needin som help to be stayin mentalee healthy,
  so each day, doze angels be re-enterin into dat Hell.

As dis uncivil war be ragin on and on,
  da medicines and bandages do rapidlee dwindle.
But Clara's angels still be much endurin,
  and defyin death's relentless duty to cull.

43. LAST BREATH

My comrade, in the next bed, wont be livin much longer.
  but I be survivin my wounds, and be gittin stronger.
Me and da nurse be prayin fur hiz peaceful everlastin.
  He be once a brave man and be savin me frum dyin.

So now da nurse iz whoevr he be wantin hur to be.
  Den she be treatin him wit hur love so mothalee.
She be wipin hiz brow and be combin hiz hair.
  Den be soothin hiz discomfort wit lovin care.

My comrade be havin no mor futur worries.
  And I be sharin wit hiz family som stories.
Hiz life shall be o'er soon. It wont be too long.
  Den he be goin, goin ... goin, gone.

44. REGIMENTAL FLAG

Thru da Wilderness dare be many shades of eye-burnin smoke,
  but I cain still be seein ar Regmental flag advancin.

Thru da deadlee struggle of bludee hand-to-hand combat,
  shall ar now-tattered flag still be a flyin?

Dat flag encourages me to be ev'n mor courageous,
  Whilst knowin scores of doze round me shall surelee die.

All too oft ar brave flag-bearers will boldlee be fallin;
  but anotha, widout hesitatin, shall hold it up high.

Shood I no longer be hearin dat drummin or de buglin,
  I be knowin my Regmental flag shall still be wavin.

45. NOT READY YET

I finalee be wakin up to be findin meself in a strange ole buildin. It be smellin like death and I be hearin awl dat cryin and moanin.

A nurse be askin me my name, but I caint yet be recallin it. Why be I in a hospital? I shood be in da van, still fightin fit.

But da doc be sayin I waz almost kilt, and shood be now dead. Seems dat I be havin a strong will to live, ev'n dough full of lead.

I be soon losin both me arms and be headin home, but wher?
I not be knowin my name or wher home iz at, tiz a godawful scare.

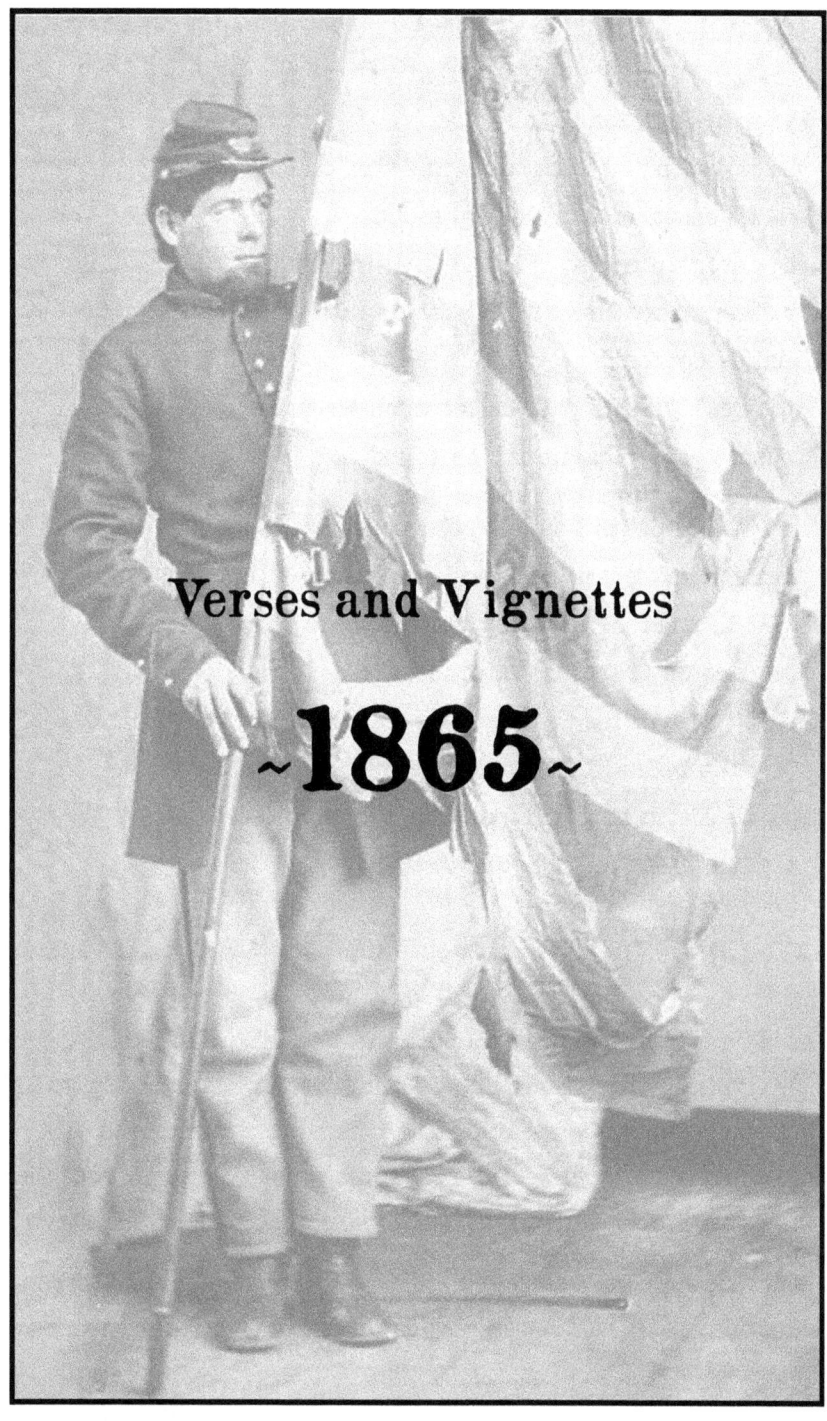

Verses and Vignettes

~1865~

46. WHAT'S IN A NAME?

Who names all doz battles done?
  Do it depend on whoz cause waz won, or lost?
Will da historians of de winnin side
  be determinin dis pridefulee namin cost?
Da Union names its battles afta da site,
  and da Confedrits by da nearest town.
Do it really matter? It be too much confusin
  whence no agreement can be found.

Tiz it to be South Mountain or Boonesboro?
  Or be it Antietam Creek or Sharpsburg?
Tiz it to be Stone River or Murfreesboro?
  Or be it da Crater or Petersburg?
Tiz it to be Shiloh Farm or Pittsburgh Landing?
  Or be it Balls Bluff or Leesburg?
And dis listin be goin on and on. History need be clear,
  tiz it a place or town, or burg?

47. GONE TOO SOON

Afta da marchin and bivouackin, and da drillin and killin,
  Billy Yank and Johnny Reb be ev'r increasin dare battle tolls.
Fur many soldiers, dare lives be endin neath som grassy knolls.
  And dem bedraggled warriors shall soon enuff becom relics of war.
Dey be havin no futurs, and dare hopes and dreams ar forevr no mor.

Doz spared wer much deformed too, becomin society's futur foragers.
  Doz once-proud men, now be miscreants, and dis war's lost wanderers.

Evry soldier be havin two lives, one befor dis war
 and one afta. And at wot cost?
Too many be ne'er havin dat later life,
 dare legacies shall hopfulee n'er be lost.
Still, we be marchin and bivouackin, drillin and killin.

48. BELLE BOYD

Miss Belle, my antebellum lover, iz amazinlee excitin.

Wit hur provocative fan tricks, tiz very much invitin.

She be devotedlee supportin da Confedrit South.

And extracts ar Union secrets wit hur sensuous mouth.

To hur, ainy means be fair by engagin love in war,
Wit ainy overheard orders dey be causin death by da score.

I be trulee lovin dat lady wit all my heart and lost soul
But now I be payin de ultimate price fur my treasonous role.

Morrow, by decree, I will be hangin in dat ole prison yard.
But I dint ev'r compromise hur. Why do I so loyalee guard?

Yet, I be a fool to be wonderin who she be wit tonite?
Probablee wit anotha Yank, reducin hiz will to fight.

49. PRISON CAMP

(A camp guard sargent overhears a conversation.)

Private, we be needin to talk! I be hearin som gossip bout you latelee. So wots on yur mind?

> Sargent, I do be havin som concerns. Why do we be treatin dem Reb traitors so well?

Tiz ar camp rules, and tiz also da right thing to be doin.

> In Andersonville, ar boyz aint gittin 3 meals a day, dare be no beds or blankets, dey be always outside freezin or sweatin, and derz no hospital fur da sicklee ones.

Dats true. But here, at Fort Delaware, we be not wantin ar prisoners to die of ainy dezeaze or hunger. We want'em to know dat bein a Union prisoner aint so bad. Maybe dey surrender, radder dan be killin ar boys.

> Sarge, dey keep killin off ar boys by 4 times az many in Andersonville, and ar Colored Troopers always be gittin shot dead ev'n if dey be surrenderin.

Yep, I be hearin dat too.

> Why caint me and a som otha guards be takin dem Rebs out fur a walk, and we cain be teachin'em som manners?

I be knowin wot you be meanin, and no, dat aint gunna be happenin on my watch.

> And dat skunk officer at Andersonville, wot say yawl bout him? We caint be doin nothin!

Furst, I be havin ya demoted and put in da brig fur insubordination. Private, I bein yur Sergeant, and yur lack of respect iz bein dulee noted. Next, I be transferrin you off to da van. Den yawl cain kill all dem Rebs on de frontlines.

Sorry Sir. I now be understandin you. But why aint dare no mor prisoner swaps?

I be seein all doz prison camp reports. We be catchin o'er 400,000 Rebs; and dey bout 200,000 Yanks. De Confedrits wood be makin out good on dat swap. And Private, why you be havin so much hate in yur heart?

Dem Rebs kilt my two older brodders at Antietam Creek. And I be sayin an eye fur an eye.

Ar doz Reb prisoners here? You be honest wit me boy.

No, but I do be lookin at all dem priznor records. And so far, nun frum Sharpsburg.

Private, I be makin a difrent point now. In '63, dare waz a smallpox sickness here, and most all doz prizoners and guards be dyin. Dey ar all buried out back. Dat epidemic to me waz much like dem senior officers frum both da North and da South tryin to git us all all kilt fur dare own damn vanity.

And anotha point. We ar goin to win dis war. Whence I be not knowin. I be believin dis cuz da Union army be havin mor men, mor guns, and we now be havin doze fightin Genrals who cain be makin dat happen. Yur choice iz to be stayin here and jest be doin yur duty or be forcin me to be sendin you South. To perhaps be kilt. Understand?

> Yes, Sarge, I do be now understandin. And I be tryin to cool my anger. But tiz hard fur me to do.

You better do. It be shameful to be havin you executed fur bein stupid. Once ar Union army frees doze survivin prisoners in Andersonville, I be hopin dat evil Warden Wirz will git noose-hung by a Union miltary tribunal.

> But dat not be enuff sir! Wirz be given dem orders, but tiz hiz guards dat did da beatin and starvin and killin!

All I cain say iz jest do yur job. Private, I be expectin nothin less. Do not be disappointin me. I be keppin my eye on you. Yur dismist.

50. HOPING FOR A TOMORROW

Az de cannons git louder, I be short of my cap and powder.
   but wit my trusty Springfield at me side, I be battle redee
At times, I be harkenin back to da huzzah cheers and back-home tears.
   I be wishin my killin hands wood now be mor steadee.

Last night, I finalee be rollin som winnin dice,
   but shood I be expectin to be da morrows sacrifice?

Shood I realee worry bout anotha battlefield loss,
  to doze unrelentin boys of Spanish moss?

Alwayz a chance my hopes cood soon com asunders,
  cuz of ainy arrogant officer's tactical blunders.
Am I to be mor of dis army's cannon fodder,
  and den jest to be my mothas boy-martyr?

Tonite, I be stackin dem hot-barrelled rifles agin,
  and tiz sad if we be havin mor weapons dan men.
Later, I agin be rollin dice and eatin cold stew,
  befor de-licin my uniform and writin home too.

If still alive, doz not wounded be gatherin fur reveille's call,
  and we den be off huntin doz Rebs behine ev'ry tree or wall.
Will my war den be o'er? Cuz fur too many, dat shall surelee be true.
  Or shall I jest be wounded befor da next mornin dew?

If alive, I be chasin doz Rebs back to da Rio Grande River.
  we be huntin em down and dare be nowher fur Johnny to shelter.
If I be dead, my comrades will be fighin till dis war iz finalee o'er.
  if lucky, dare be no back-home tears. Huzzah, da Union forev'r!

51. ALL EQUAL NOW

Chancellorsville and Chantilly, Bull Run and Shiloh,
  wher West Point friends and rivals be meetin befo.

Both Johnston and Jackson be takin a southern oath,
  and be dyin befo dare times, American traitors both.

Yet, dey wer courageous leaders, yet full of treason,.
  and did die earlee deaths be fur dat very reason?

Both Kearney and Stevens be dyin too in Hell's fiery breech,
   but dey be tryin to preserve da Union, twas dare mission each.

Der deaths wer due to McClellan bein a poor tactical leader,
   and in time, Lincoln's new genrals won victories in evry theatre.

Death be God's great equalizer wit da dirt be reclaimin us awl,
   cuz yur cause, rank, valor, or wealth be meanin nothin at awl.

Chancellorsville and Chantilly, Bull Run and Shiloh.
   Wher West Point friends and rivals be meetin befo.

52. 100 MILES

Wit Washington and Richmond jest bein one hunderd miles apart,
   a bold southern Confederacy of States did a secession start.
Doz slave-ownin leaders declared its 'secund war fur independance,'
   cuz dey be tired of doze northern brothas' hypocrisy and arrogance.

Doz Rebels also be callin it dare 'war against yankee agression,'
   whilst dem Union leaders be callin it dare 'war aginst secession.'
No mattered de battle cries, da Union waz tryin to persevere,
   and called upon its state gov'nors to git its menfolk to volunteer.

Whence bludee civil war tween brothas at Fort Sumpter begins,
   der waz to be no peace till one side, or de otha, decisivelee wins.
Az de ne'r endin list of battles be increasin wit its casualties galore,
   newspapers be listin da dead at de Wilderness, da Crater, and mor.

Twas tragic dis war tween sista States waz so bitterly fought.
   life lost its value; but wit Union blood, its preservation waz bought.

Wit Washington and Richmond jest bein one hunderd deadly
  miles apart,
Som in da South still be sowin seeds of hate. To be wantin
  anotha start?

53. TRAITOR

Jefferson Davis to be leeden doz southern states to secede,
  and den da war beginned at Sumpter suddenlee.
Dis tragedy be leavin Dixie families destitute,
  and losin dare confederit dignitee.
But dare hatred still be thrivin,
  so ar Union must still be on guard eternally.

54. ONE SOLDIER'S PRAYER

Dearest Lord, derz much to do today unda dis ole magnolia tree,
  I now be prayin.
Here, a once-proud plantation slaver be doin hiz tobac smokin
  and bourbon sippin.
Den afta long hot days of over-seein da cotton pickin
  and hiz darkie back-lashin.
We be buryin him soon, and hopin he be facin Hell's fury.
  In Thy name, I be Amenin.

55. COLORED TROOPS
(A Union soldier praises the resolve of Darkie soldiers.)

At furst, doz darkie soldiers wer ordered
   to jest be used in non-fightin roles;
But dey went on to be symbolizin da hopes
   of dem enslaved southern souls.
Frum carpenters and cooks, scouts and spies, guards
   and doze tireless tasks az laborers,
To bein miltary steamboat pilots, battlefield surgeons,
   and dependable yankee fighters.
Afta provin demselves at da Wagner Battery Battle,
   de 54th Mass waz most brave.
Fur many a colored troopers felt da heat of battle,
   and wit Shaw, be enterin a massiv grave.
Sargent Carney waz da furst Medal of Honor
   fur a darkie soldier's valiant ferocitee,
And den fourteen mor colored troopers
   wer such medal-awarded fur dare battle gallantree.
Doze battles at Big Cabin, Honey Springs, Port Hudson
   and othas had dem Rebs flee.
Da heart of de 54th den be dashin awl de futur hopes
   of dat southern confedricy.
By da surrender of Lee at Appomattox,
   bout 200-thouzund colored troopers wer in dis fight.
Dats mor men dan awl da Rebel Army be havin,
   dat wer now in a backward flight.
Huzzah to doze 40-thouzund Colored Troopers dat died,
   I be today honorin yawl

You be heppin preserve dis Union; and we be prayin
   you soon be fulfillin yur hopes awl.
Doz Colored Troops cain soon be leadin da way
   fur educatin dare yung.
Whilst dare futur tiz still uncertain,
   at least dis effort haz now begun.
De African contraband must be havin its special place
   in dis Union's futur,
Az long az da fedral North cain be keepin its promises,
   year afta year afta year.

56. LOST SOUL
(A soldier has post-war problems.)

Hiz boyhood twas lost, and at wot cost?
No mo huntin and no mo fishin.
No mo schoolin and no mo spoonin.
Too much left unsaid.

He be lovin hiz State trulee, and be hatin dat enemy unrulee.
Sadlee dis nation iz divided, wit too much to be decided.
He enlisted and drilled, fought well and killed.
Den he be left fur dead.

Az a maimed vetran, he be wishin to be in heaven.
He slept oft and be stayin unkept, az hiz famlee sadlee wept.
Dis oft medalled lad be left feelin so alone and quite sad.
Twas now hard to show love, so he n'er be wed.

He be too much drinkin and too much brawlin.
And too much rantin and too much ragin.
Jest, too much too muchin. Wit no good-byin,
He den gun-kilt hizself. Nuff said.

57. BREEDING BARN

Why buy'em when you cain breed'em and sell'em,
  if I aint be seein it, I aint be believin it.
We Yankee boys be seein dem southern manshuns gleamin,
  wit doze yung darkie gurls be fearin to alwayz be breedin.

In doze big southern famlee farms, dey be callin a plantation,
  doze slave-owners be disgraceful in dis war-shredded nation.

Som of dem plantations be like som godless fancy gal brothels,
  wit contraband gurls bein legal-raped by som scoundrels.

Dem gurls bein torn frum dare families, or bein sold to othas,
  it be causin da deepest pain to doz helpless fathas and mothas.
I be havin a yunger sista, and she be not lika horse or cow,
  to be birthin babies to be later slave-workin a plough.

Now I be fightin fur da Union and not jist my sista,
  I be fightin to lance dis shamful breedin blister.
So now, no mo buy'em, breedin'em or sell'em,
  if I aint be seein it, I aint be believin it.

58. LITTER BEARERS

Me and my darkie friend, ole Tom, we be two litter bearers on the battlefront. I be too yung to be fightin, but not too old to be willinlee heppin. We be shuttlin doz wounded Union soldiers to de nearby field hospital and to be carryin doz specialee dat cood not be walking so well. Dis time, de hospital iza huge and empty farmhouse wit many windows. Dis place be full of beds fur da wounded to hepp dem purposefulee.

Me and ole Tom be watchin ole sawbones fixin up doz damaged bodies, by cuttin off dare mutilated limbs, but not too visedlee. Doz arms and legs wer den throwed outta dem wide and shuttered windows. And we wood den proper cover'em thorolee. Later, me and Tom be carryin ainy bodyless limbs to da trench down da road. Den we will do shallow bury'em, most revrentlee. Dat smell waz unforgetablee bad.

Whence returnin, we be carryin mo and mo wounded to doz bloodied tables, and ole sawbones be givin dem soldier boys som nummin whiskee to swallow quicklee. Fur doz dat lived, we be shuttlin dem down da steep and muddee path to doz big rehab tents to somhow rest and be recoverin, oft painfulee. Doz dat dint survive da sawin, we be takin dare lifeless and carved bodies to da burial ditch fur som eternal rest. Den we be prayin respectfulee fur doz soldier boys.

Me and Tom ne'r be gittin used to da warz gruesom sights, smells, and sounds. And we ne'r be forgettin dis daylee war-promised realitee. We be a good team tryin to be savin awl dem brave yankee boys in blue. So we keep re-enterin thru doz bludee gates of Hell, most dutifulee. Whilst I still be a litter bearer, yet too yung to be fightin; but old Tom aint. He now be a Union private off fightin to boldlee free dem slaves.

59. GRAND REVIEW

I be comin home Maw, comin home Paw,
   and hopin to see dat stubborn mule wid its ole hee-haw.
I soon be findin out wot dis sad war wazabout.
   And am glad tiz now o'er, dare aint no doubt.
I shot me som Rebs, and dey shot me too.
   So wots a one-legged vetran goin to now do?
I be crutchin my way to da train station square,
   and git me in line wit de otha boys dare.
Soon den I be huggin my Maw, huggin my Paw,
   and huggin dat mule wit its ole hee-haw.

Den I be soon allowin my fallen comrades to be stayin alive thru me.
   And be honorin dem by bein az happy and futur content az I cain be.
Dis war be teachin me much bout meself, az well az som othas.
   I be wunderin whence awl dem rebel soldiers cain agin be brothas.

Der be no Grand Review marchin fur me, and doze othas like me. But dats okay fine. I now be gettin stronger, tiz my main priority. I be most grateful fur discoverin a new life. Hopin to be renewed. I also be hopin to find a lovin wife and be startin a brood. Huzzah!

~ Soldier Recollections ~

60. JACOB

(A private remembers his former sargent talking about a dependable corporal.)

Accordin to my ole sargent, he be knowin Jacob az one of hiz mor reliable corprals. Jacob waz knowd to da sargent and me az a shy, strong son of a Kentuckee farmer. Den bout ten and eight months later, Jacob waz a battle-scared vetran soldier huddlin in a shallow ditch near doze Chatnooga mountens. Seems lika lifetime ago when da sargent be tellin me about hiz last encounter wit da corporal …

… Whilst preparin fur combat in dis mounten valley, Jacob, long wit hiz shaggy company comrades be restin by da edge of a large and forebodin meddow. In dis unfamiliar spot of terra firma, wher da weak cold sun barelee be risin bove da horizon, doze blustery days seem endlesslee bleak and lackin of color. He be shiverin wit hiz soldier possoms in dis pock-marked land of black and white, and awl gray shades tween. Dis vetran cood not be imaginin why dis field lay so barren, even though tiz wintertime. He oft be crouchin, and ponderin bout hiz life, in dis snake pit of war.

Rememberin home, Jacob reckoned a fallow field shood be havin som sort of life, or even bearin som markins of a plough. Dis once-green meddow appeared to be ne'r been autumn-ploughed, or at all. In da once-dense forest surroundin dis snow-covered field stood bones of trees dat had surlee leafed and bloomed befo.

On dis frozen field, wher da trees lay like corpses, twas hard fur him to be envisionin dat ainy spring or summer season had ev'r be visitin dis expansive place, now draped in perpetual gloom. Dis drizzlee gloom had invaded hiz soul, and in da souls of many othas az well. Afta doze days of dreadful marchin and defence-buildin, he waz too tired to be sleepin and too hungry to be eatin. Hiz mind oft wandered off, usualee homeward, wher life waz less harsh.

He be respondin to da plea of hiz State Guvnor to eagerlee be joinin hiz friends and neighbors to be fightin in dis patriotic war. We be tryin to save ar way of life, and dey be tryin to be savin derz. Tho bein a young lad, he knowd himself to be an able hunter. Jacob's aim waz true befor enlistin, and it twaz still, in dis cold and hostile mounten forest of impendin agony. He waz yunger dan most of doze otha recruits, da army be orderin him to train doze less skilled in de weapons of war.

Befo, Jacob be dailee ploughin and harvestin longside hiz fatha fur years and years. Dat made him strong and robust. And dare waz no time fur ainy idleness or sloth. No time ev'n fur hizelf. So, whence da civil war waz furst declared, he saw hiz big chance to break wit hiz farmin ruteens. He be cravenin to see mor dan jest doze acres he be workin on fur years.

Afta enlistin, Jacob waz in jest two shakes on a slow-movin troop-train headin to a miltary trainin camp. Three winters befo, Jacob's fatha had unexpectedly died frum da black measles, leavin him to care fur hiz motha, da yunger ones, and de family farm. Twas a lot to be shoulderin, but he be provenin hizelf to be most able. Long wit hiz yunger brotha, Luke, dey be managin to be yieldin mor crops dan hiz fatha ev'r had. Twaz a point of family pride. But twas hiz time to be movin on. Da army be needin him.

Luke waz two years yunger; but Jacob be knoin hiz brotha cood, probablee in time, be able to be takin care of hiz motha and doze three younger sisters. Luke waz an out-goin, good-natured lad whooz taller and much stronger dan Jacob ev'r waz. Whilst Jacob waz shy, hiz brotha waz not. Still, he oft be wonderin if hiz brotha waz up to awl doze relentless farmin tasks. Dats wot big brothas be doin, dey worry.

A gust of blustery wind startlin Jacob back into hiz current sad reality. He be needin to discreetlee to be movin hiz oft stiffenin body into difrent positions. Da stingin sleetee cold had seeped into hiz arms and legs. He waz numbed frum sittin in ainy one position too long. Da battle-exhausted company had been in dare defensive positions fur countless days. Jest waitin fur somthin to be happenin, dat only dare officers must be knowin. Dey not be receivin no orders to fur advancin; but dem officers oft be orderin da company's men to be keepin low to da ground, to be movin only a lil bit, and to be az quiet az possible. If dey had a call of nature, dey wood be slowly crawlin away into a once-dense grove of leafless and lifeless trees wher da smelly open latrine waz hidin and to den be returnin silentlee. And whenced halted, to be revealin da proper password to avoid bein shot dead. One caint be too careful in war.

Jacob alwayz be followin hiz orders faithfulee, but today waz difrent. Twas suddenlee cold and windy. Hiz fingers and toes wer gittin mor nummer. Twas it dat damned frostbite agin? If so, he cood be loosin som fingers or toes. He be hopin not, since dare aint no sanitary units near. Wit vigor, he be rubbin hiz hands on hiz thighs, be tirelesslee blowin on hiz frozen fingers, and be tryin to wiggle hiz now bluein toes.

Dare aint nothin seemed to be workin. Hiz pain increased mo and mo. Twas becomin unbearable. Lookin across dat empty meddow, he wondered if hiz enemy waz still on dare otha side of dis remote no-man's land. Jest like us, do dey also be crouchin low, and be freezin?

Aint been no sign of dare movment fur sevral uncounted days. Wer dey still ther? Or did dey jest be secretlee packin up and bein gone? Den Jacob's company of begrimed men wood be alone and isolated, to be jest sittin in dis bitter weather, and be hidin frum no one.

He cood not suffer bein motionless ainy longer. Jacob be lowerin hiz head, and be struglin to take off hiz icy, woollen cap. It be frozen to hiz wavee hare. He be rigruslee scratchin hiz oily-matted scalp. Twas it dat damned head lice agin? He be hopin not. Or wazzit jest hiz livelee magination? Whence Jacob did sleep, he oft be havin dem nitemarish dreams.

Afta re-securin hiz frosty cap back onto hiz head, he be vigruslee rubbin hiz filthy hands togetter agin and agin. Twas hard to keep hiz cold blood circulatin. If he waz home, wot wood he be doin? Hiz mind be wanderin off agin.

At da farmstead, Jacob waz alwayz dutifulee up at dawn; and jest be workin, eatin, and peein befor dinner time. Somtimes, durin a sunny day, he be talkin to dem yung local girls who did somtimes be strollin passed da farm. Dey wer alwayz wearin dare well-washed homemade dresses wit colorful bonnets. Somtimes, one wood be bringin him a warm, freshly-baked cake. He be likin da apple ones da most. One of dem pretty girls dint quite fit in. She dint wear a fancy dress. She be wearin som workin trousers and a floppy straw-hat. Hur smile be catchin Jacob's eye. She be havin a wonderful smile. Rememberin dis did brieflee bring him great joy. She be shy, jest like he be.

Jacob oft be wonderin if ainy of doze girls be missin him now, especialee da one wit dat big floppy straw-hat. Wot ar dey goin to do wit him gone frum hiz farm? Whooz gonna eat awl doze mouth-waterin cakes? Twas hiz volunteerin to fight da right thing to do? Yep, no question. But it be nicer havin dat special girl waitin fur him to be comin back home.

Well, he caint be worrin bout dat now. Jacob's prioritee was to be stayin alive and to be killin de enemy. And to also hep hiz comrades be stayin alive too.

Why did dis war tween da North and South be havin to go on so long? Much longer dan ainy be thinkin. If Jacob had been older, mor wiser and experienced, wood he be knowin wot doz genrals be expectin? It dint madder. Dis war iz behavin like it be havin its own life.

Jacob's once spit-polished boots wer now well-worn and mud-caked. Hiz once spotless uniform waz now soiled and bullet-torn. Lucklee jest a minor wound. Hiz rifle and bayonet wer rusty and needin to be cleaned and oiled ev'ry day in dis cold and damp mounten valley. And to be keepin alert by keepin hiz body movin.

Befo, dare be som minor skirmishes. Twas a great relief frum doze bloody slaughters of earlyer battles. He be hearin dat war waz Hell. Ev'n dough dis part of Hell waz now freezin. Lucklee, in dis mounten cold, ainy dead bodies wood not be heat-bloated and explodin, and den spewin dem smelly innards awl o'er da parched earth.

Afta doz summer battles, Jacob be promoted to corporal. He waz already handlin dis kind of added duties. Yet, in battle, Jacob dint know if he had actualee kilt anyone. Whilst once a crack-shot, Jacob waz now jest shootin blindlee and reloadin quicklee. Jest shoot and reload, shoot and reload, az fast az he cood. Twas real frustratin.

Nowadays, da billowin clouds wer possessed by a thick fog or icy rain. A fog so thick Jacob cood not hardlee be seein hiz own boots. At dawn and dusk, twas ev'n mor difcult to see. awl hiz targets be seemin mor ghostlee in da fog, smoke, and chaos. He wood continue to shoot hiz rifle in de direction of ainy noise or movment; and be hopin to hear a whimper or a moan. Still, he cood be tellin hiz army stories back home wher hiz farmer friends wood be listenin, and perhaps som pretty girls too. Especialee da one wit dat straw-hat.

Jacob be decidin to marry hur afta dis war ended. Hur birthname waz Elizabeth Anne; but he alwayz be callin hur Betsy. He dint realee know if she be feelin da same way. Or dat she be findin anotha farmer boy whilst he waz in dis war far away? Jacob oft said to me dat, 'Sarge, if I be goin to die, I wood ratter die in hur arms at home dan in dis god-forsaken, misty mounten meddow.'

Jacob be needin to agin be shiftin hiz sittin position to relieve a cramp or two, or three. He waz so sick and tired of hiddin in dis muddy clay ditch. He be thinkin dat jest pigs sit in dis mud. But not him! I be a soldier, not a mud-sittin, fightin man! Rememberin hiz fatha's voice, 'Son, I'd radder be kilt by a dam bullet dan die by som swamp or mounten bug.'

Jacob den leant o'er to tighten and re-tie hiz mud-soaked boots. Anythin now be better dan jest sittin and fretin. We be here doin nothin. Twas tired of awl dis shiftin and waitin. Dis shiftin and waitin waz makin him crazy. Ainy able-bodied vetran shood not be waitin to be rescued by som warmer summer weather in dis hellish place. Afta awl, dey wer awl well-trained and vetran fightin men. He be needin to be doin somthin portant. To be actin soon, and to be actin decisivelee!

He be stretchin out hiz crampin legs az carefulee az he cood, witout standin up. Witout ainy sound, and witout drawin ainy attention. Jacob be believin he waz fulee protected by hiz own special massive branchless tree, perhaps felled by som brutal wind, or by age. But mor likelee felled by a misdirected enemy shell earlier in da war. Lookin round, he be noticin dare waz som moss growin on hiz ole dead tree, wit som slimy mushrooms peekin out round it. So, life still do be existin here in dis no-man's land! A nice surprize. Lil things can madder in war. He den be spottin som lichen on a shattered stump of da lone branch on hiz tree. It be crumblin unda da touch of hiz cold and gnarled fingers. He be wipin off its debris on hiz pant leg. Life iz so dear, no matter where it be found.

Jacob be peerin o'er hiz sacred ground-huggin tree dat still be protectin him frum da winter's ravagin wind. He be knowin dis tree also be protectin him frum dat ghost army frum de otha side of da meddow. Dis one very special rottin tree be keepin Jacob frum venturin out to dat ice-crusted field, and to perhaps not be yellin madlee or be firin hiz weapon wildlee. By now, he waz dead-sur hiz enemy had abandoned dare side of no-man's land. dare be no sights or sounds in mor dan a week or so.

Cood he now be releasin som bottled-up tensions wit som hootin and shootin? Nobody o'er dare wood ev'n notice him. O'er der, only a foolish foe-man wood still be crouchin quietlee in dis cold and godforsaken earth. Maybe da only fools left in dis meddow wer hiz own bedeviled Company. Wer Jacob and hiz begrimed comrades da only ones dare? Doze once-gallant enemy ghosts wer now cowardlee gone! Or smartlee gone?

Fur days, da sun be failin to break thru doze foggy thick clouds. Like magic dare be one brite ray of sunshine be dat be escapin the fog, awl by itself. It be zigzaggin its way cross de open ground. Did ainy otha soldiers be seein dis amazin sunbeam? Bein mesmerized by its dazlin rays, Jacob be watchin it spark up som small patches of dead grass, once partlee hidden by a threadbare sheet of ice.

Da increasin light of dis lonesom sunbeam waz meanderin slowlee cross no-man's land. Here and dare, its bright flare wood be reflectin off som shiny relic of a past battle's debris. dare be no one venturin out on dis meadow, at least not afta hiz company had positioned itself countless days ago.

Jacob agin be lookin round at hiz weary warrior friends. Most wer lyin wit dare backs aginst dare own headstones of fallen trees. Either dey be readin som well-worn books or be writin letters home. Som men wer sleepin soundlee. He too be needin to be finishin som letters. Had no one else be seein dis special ray of sunshine? Had no one else be experiencin dis rare chance fur som unpredicted joy? Too late now, da sunbeam be suddenlee disappearin, jest az it had suddenlee be appearin. He be hopin it waz not jest a daydream. Jacob's nite terrors had now been visitin him mor frequentlee and in the daytime too.

Dis sunbeam be bringin him great joy and wunderment in dis godforsaken place. Hiz joy waz now becomin uncontainable, uncontrollable. He waz unexpectedlee happy and calm. Hiz entire body be takin on a life of its own. No mor waz hiz pain felt, and he waz no longer cold. Strange, but soothin. Jacob den be startin hiz hee-haw dancin and singin az if he waz attendin a back-home barn dance.

Only den did he be aware of hiz comrades be hollarlin fur him to git down. But he waz revellin in de new awareness dat hiz warmin blood waz now flowin into hiz sore and tired legs. He be stretchin out hiz once heavy and achy arms az he be grinin at da soldier be gesturin fur him to git down.

Suddenlee outta da corner of hiz eye, Jacob den be spottin a flicker of light, a silent flash. Az he turnin round to better see … ZZZZT! He be feelin a severe blow to hiz gut. Twas like a mad mule had jest be kickin him hard. He be den doublin o'er and fallin backwards o'er da log dat had earlyer been protectin him.

Az he be layin dare bewildered, he den be witnessin hiz life's blood oozin out o'er hiz uniform, like a thick crimson lava flow. Hiz pain waz deep and searin, like a brandin iron be sizzlin inside hiz chest.

From nowher, no-man's land be eruptin into thunderous noise and mayhem. Frum dare, well-hidden enemy cannons now be roarin wit its lethal shells whistlin overhead. Life-takin weapons be rippin up da earth in front of Jacob's comrades. De rifle fire waz much intense frum both sides of dat once silent mounten meddow. Shells wer explodin and causin geysers of dirt and limbs.

Jacob cood no longer be hearin de blastin sounds or da powdery smells of da battle. Hiz vision waz gittin blurry, and hiz breathin waz gittin wheezy. Jacob waz much confused. Hiz world be collapsin behine hiz once-proud and now-hallowed tree. He becomed keenlee aware dat hiz bug-filled log wit its greenish moss, yellowy mushrooms, and silvery lichen wer still alive. Whilst he waz certainlee dyin. Wer dey weepin fur him? Da whole of Jacob's body waz becomin num and hiz final thoughts be homeward bound … to hiz motha, to hiz brotha and sistas, to doze apple pies, and to …

Afta endless hours of shell-shockin noise and destruction, da moanin of doze wounded and dyin went quiet. An eerie quiet. Dis pulverized battlefield den be revealin Jacob's survivin comrades. Dey had decided who wood be bringin hiz lifeless body back frum no-man's land. Who wood be sendin back personal items back to hiz heartland home. And who wood be ensurin hiz burial place be honorablee marked. Dey awl be knowin Jacob wood be respectfulee fare-welled later, in dis cursed land of combat.

Once hiz company comrades had reverentlee completed dare solemn afta-battle duties, one soldier be hesitantlee mentionin dat he be hearin

som of Jacob's words last muttered. Som otha comrades also be hearin somthin az well. Togetter, dey recollected a few probable words. One battle-worn comrade believed he be hearin one-word clearlee; but it dint be makin ainy sense. Dat word bein "straw-hat." …

… *Az Jacob's Sargent and friend, I volunteered fur dat sorrowful honor of returnin Jacob's personals to hiz heartland farm. And to personalee be hand-deliverin hiz unfinished letter to Miss Betsy, az he had befor promised. Whilst in Kentuck, I be meetin wit Jacob's family; and be tellin dem bout dare brave son. Dey awl cried uncontrollablee, me too. And waz den told dat Betsy waz married and wit-child, agin. Twas also told dat hur baby girl's name waz Jacobina. I den be thinkin I shood not be deliverin Jacob's last letter to Betsy. I be decidin now to cowardlee give dis letter to Jacob's motha instead. She cood den do wots best. Jacob's mother can destroy it or sav it. It be hur decision, not mine. My unfulfilled promise left me feelin bittersweet. But Jacob's final chapter waz done, and Betsy's next chapter waz jest beginin. And I be knowin Jacob wood be okay wit dat.*

61. SOONER OR LATER

Befo da war, I be havin a great many hopes and aspirashuns,
  so I wood den ratter be dyin much later, dan mor sooner.
Durin da war, I be smellin and seein too many abominashuns,
  so I wood den ratter be dyin much sooner, dan mor later.
Afta da war, I be havin so many of life's gloryus obligashuns,
  so I wood now ratter be dyin much later, dan mor sooner.

62. COMPANY LIFE
(A Federal Army private remembers.)

I be enlistin in da U.S. Army durin de spring of '60, and be proudlee joinin da regular Army, II Corps. I waz already aginst southern slavery like many otha northerners. I be believin to my core dat awl people be created equal. And I be commendin John Brown's efforts at startin dat slave insurrection. Da time fur talk had sadlee passed. And in dis army, I be havin som good lodgin, eatin dailee meals and wearin a uniform blue. I also be needin to earn som money too fur my family back home.

Bein an Army reglar be givin me som feelin of importance; and I be meetin otha soldiers wit da same views. My furst army order waz to be protectin da same armory at Harper's Ferry dat Brown be surrenderin in befor. Twas spooky. dare I be learnin to drill and to be earnin my miltary dues. In early '61, I be transferin to Fort Ripley in Minisota to be protectin doze brave settlers movin west. Dem injuns wer alwayz in da way.

Den da Civil War be startin whence doze rebs be startin to cannon shell Fort Sumpter. Da rebellion tween da States begun dat day. Dis war waz not civil at all.

By July '61, we be leavin fur D.C. to be joinin up wi McDowell's Potomac Army, and to be battle-drillin unda da most hot sun. Som comrades be dyin in trainin. Early in '62, I becamed a proud member of Hunter's Division, Porter's Brigade. And soon we be marchin to Bull Run. I waz in Company C of da 2nd Regiment. Ar furst battle waz so disorderlee dat I thought I be losin my will to be in da Fedral Army. Twas scared fur my life. But afta recoverin frum dat shame, I be heppin train doze new recruits to be preparin fur da chaos of battle.

To stop de advancin Confedrit Army, Company C lost many a good man at Yorktown and Mechanicsville. And lost mor brave souls at Gainesville, Antietam Creek, 2nd Bull Run, Shepherdstown, Fredericksburg, and Malvern Hill. De death dint ev'r end. Den oft in da front ranks of da van, waz not much in da rearguard. Dem officers cood alwayz be countin on us Company C boys. I be proud of dat. Twas difcult explainin da butchery and mayhem to doze new recruits. Dey learnt to be expectin each day to be dare last. I jest be doin my duty and followin orders, no madder how good or bad dey be.

Fightin in '63 waz not much difrent. Exceptin twas mor deadlee. But mercifulee, I be survivin. Company C agin fought well at Chancellorsville, Gettysburg, and Bristol Station; and I be wounded agin and agin, but not too severelee.

Fightin in '64 waz a bit difrent. Da South now be knowin it waz losin da war. And so doze battles becomed much mor savage. Dem secesh genrals be showin us no mercy, specialee dem Colored soldiers. Company C took ev'n mor losses in da Wilderness, Spotsylvania, North Anna, and in de Totopotomoy carnages. Afta losin many a good friend, I be findin it hard to be startin new friendships.

Besides my many wounds, I also be catchin som swamp poxes. Many soldier possums wood be dyin of dare wounds or of da fever. But I dint. Once recoverin, I be fightin agin at Cold Harbor, Petersburg Crater, and Peebles Farm. Wood dis slaughterin e'er stop? Dis proud and once-larger Company be reduced to bout 100 good and healthy fightin men frum its beginin number.

In June of '64, dis horror of war finalee be endin fur us. We survivin soldiers took part in da transfer to Elmira, in New York. Twas much relieved. In October of '64, we be transferin agin. Dis time back to da Newport Barracks, in Kentuck. And den in April of '65, we be hearin of Lee's Surrender. Huzzah! In da fall of '65, my Company C waz agin transfered. So off we be goin to da Crittenden Barracks, in Injiana. We jest had to be endurin awl dem transfers to nowher portant. I be gittin tired of awl dis travellin back and forth, back and forth. Twas den mentalee spent and my body waz a wreck.

It waz finalee time fur me to be movin on to a new life. On reflectin, I waz proud of my role in Company C. We awl be livin up to de Company motto of '*Noli Me Tangere*' … do not be tamperin or messin or medlin or interferin wit us. To me, it jest be meanin, 'get outta ar way yawl or you be havin a deadlee price to pay!'

Dis Army life aint no longer be appealin to me. Yet mor othas be stayin in da reglar Army since dat war be endin. But not me. Dey be headin west to be fightin dem injuns. Dis be meanin to burn down der tent villages and to be killin awl survivors. I be not wantin to do dat. So den by horse, I be ridin back home slow; and den be makin a new life fur meself.

Erelong I be workin hard az a wagon-maker. But still be havin doze scary nite terrors. Whence I ev'r recover? Probably not dat soon. Many otha vetrans ar jest like me, spooked. I once be fightin hard and be survivin, whilst many othas dint. Som of da Company C survivors jest becomed da livin dead. Dey be wanderin frum town to town, job to job. Fur dem, nothin shall e'er be az befor.

We be savin dis Union and be makin sur dat slavry be endin. But now, both da nation and me be needin to git reconciled. Fur me, de end of dis war waz not de end of da battle inside me head. It still be hard to be livin and workin. I be hopin dat o'er time, I be adjustin to my new life. It will be hard cuz I be too proud and too scared to be sharin my feelins wit othas. Yet, I be knowin dat life do go on, and I must be decidin on how to be livin in it.

63. COMRADES REUNITE
(A diary entry of a Union Army veteran after the 50th Anniversary of the Gettysburg battle.)

Tonite, I be writin bout my experiences frum da day's reunion,
  Whence many vetrans be showin off dare past battlefield pride.
Twas brought to tears many times durin dat solemn ceremony.
  Awl dat '63 death iz still very real fur me. I still be raw inside.
I caint brin myself to be shakin da hands of doz Reb vetrans attendin.
  So, I be leavin dis event recallin too many a comrade dat died.
Othas be wantin me forgivin and forgettin. But I be not ready fur dat yet.
  I caint betray my fallen friends, ev'n whilst we survivors ar now few.
So I be patrollin doze sacred grounds, wher dem new monuments now stand.
  And doze hallowed headstones be shadin dis now green and peaceful land.
Whilst I waz pausin to reflect, I be hearin a once-familiar voice …
  'Hey Worm, iz dat you? Yes, it must be you! Iz dat true?'
Lordee, it be him! My ole Company Corporal who be callin me 'Bookworm.'
  And iz hiz ghost now appearin? Should I be much scared and fearin?

I den be callin him 'Corpse.' He be savin me frum death many a time befor.
    But dare he be slumpinlee standin, Corporal Corpse, n'er agin to be disappearin.
'Is dat you possum, my own livin corpse? I reckoned you be kilt at Gettysburg!'
He almost waz; and iz now wearin hiz skewed eyepatch, much discomfortin?
He be tellin me bout dat explosion dat pilfered hiz left eye forev'r,
    And bout dat drunken surgeon dat scorched it most savagelee ruff.
Corpse be recallin ar furst meetin in '60, at Fort Ripley, in Kansas.
    Dats wher he be teachin me to be a strong soldier tuff.
He be walkin mor slowlee, tryin not to stumble. My wounds wer mor mental.
    Fur us, we both jest be survivin dez last 50 years. Twas hard enuff.
Corpse said he caint forgit da misery of dat ole brutal war gone bye.
    Cuz passin evry window or mirror reflection be remindin him.

He be savin my life one rainy day durin a hard-fought Virginie battle,
    So den I be givin Corpse my only pair of dry socks. He still got'em.
We sat quietlee on dat grassy knoll overlookin dat once deadlee field.
    Words wer not needed az ar shared past waz gladlee gittin dimmer.
Az da sun descended, we gracelesslee stood and awkwardlee hugged.
    Our ole friendship waz now re-found and thankfulee restored.
Afta som silence, Corpse went hiz way, and I be goin anotha.
    We be believin ar tears be makin us less manlee, but renewin.
We be knowin dis brief chinwag waz good medicine fur ar lost souls.
    And dis bein my last reunion, I finalee be ready fur som healin.
On da morrow, I be writin bout dis visit wit my dearest soldier friend,
    Beside sharin past life woes, we'll be friends till I be dead.

64. MATHEW OR MATTY
(A relationship between a mother and her veteran son.)

Mathew be tyin up hiz tired ole mare to a bigtooth maple and soon be walkin up da long dusty path to hiz childhood home in north Texas. He be skidish cuz he not be visitin hiz home in o'er ten seasons. De ranch dint look da same, but dats to be expected. Wots dat o'er dare, jest right of de house? It be lookin like two headstones hidin in a copse of oak trees. He mite be walkin o'er dare later.

Dis homecomin cood be complicated. Hiz mind waz beginin to wonder... Twas only a lad of 17 years whence ridin north to be joinin da Fedral army. Afta enlistin in '58, Mathew waz furst posted to Fort Leavenworth. Earlyer, az a family, dey be leavin Georgia in da late '40s. Hiz fatha, motha, lil brotha and he, be movin westward to be startin a new life. Hiz fatha waz a fedral army soldier who proudlee be fightin in da war aginst Mexico. Hiz wounds dint slow him down much den. And dats whence hiz father fell in love wit Texas. So he be decidin to try hiz hand at ranchin. Hiz fatha waz happy, but hiz motha twas not. But she jest be gittin used to awl doz new ruteens.

Afta a long sweaty footslog, Mathew did be reachin hiz ole front porch. Mathew waz gettin nervous. Hiz war experiences and afta be makin him less carin and mo violent. He be hopin dis visit be hepin him find hiz ole self, Matty. Twas strange to knock on da same door he and Benny wer once busy runnin in and out of awl doz many years ago. He paused to be lettin hiz nerves calm down. Twas he really home? And jest befor he be knockin agin, da door be swingin open. And dare be standin hiz maw. She be shorter dan he be rememberin. And she be be wearin da same ole dress he be recallin frum befor? Hur tied-back hair be turnin gray. Otha dan dat, it waz da same ole wide smile. Now wot? Befor he cood speak, hur soft yet strong voice spooked him.

Matty, iz dat realy you? Oh my God, do com in, com in. I caint believe it, tiz realy you afta awl diz many years? How bout som coffee? I got som brewin rite now.

Hiz misgivins quicklee be meltin away. He be feelin like he jest be comin home frum skool or frum mending fences.

Maw den be scurryin off to da kitchen to be fetchin hiz coffee, and Mathew be settin down hiz heavy grip in a place jest outside on de front porch by da ole swing. Inside, he be lookin round and be seein awl de same ole fittins in de same ole place. Twas like he waz here jest yesterday. Dats whence he be spottin three daguerreotypes on de wood fireplace mantel. Dey wer of hiz fatha, hiz lil brotha, and awl three of dem togeter. But none of Mathew. Twas a strange feelin not to be part of dat groupin. Durin da war, he be seein som of doze fancy pictures; and be knowin how pricy dey wer. Den da hot coffee waz delivered, in China cups, he'd ne'r be remeberin frum before.

'Maw, I jest be seein yur daguerreotypes. So wherz Pa and Benny now? Out mindin da fences I suppose?'

Der waz a long awkward pause az she bent down az if she waz hard-kicked by a mule.

Matty, dey ar both dead. Please suffer me to be tellin you wot happened.

Afta a scant time to reflect and to gatha som forlorn calm, she begined to tell hur sorrowful story.

Furst, whence da war aginst da confedrit rebellion begined, Benny waz jest old nuff to be enlistin in da Fedral Army. And jest like you be doin in '58. So, in '62, he be ridin off on hiz well-packed horse headin north to be joinin da 1st Arkansaw Union Infantry. In Texas, dare waz only secesh miltary units nearby. Yur fatha be insistin dat Benny be fightin fur da Union. And very soon afta hiz trainin, he waz quick kilt by som rebs in '63 in da battle of Haguewood Prairie, tis somwher in Arkansaw. Yur fatha and me wer heart-broken and be placin a headstone near da back of de house. It be one of Benny's favored spots. But Benny aint buried ther, tiz only an immortelle, wotev'r dat iz. Den in '64, yur fatha died of a pox dat waz passin thru Texas. He waz weaklee befo, and twas ne'r de same afta Benny waz kilt by dem Rebs. Mo like dyin of a broken heart.

Mathew be thinkin bout both fatha and Benny bein dead. Too much to be ponderin rite now. Dat be explainin doze two headstones bein out back.

'Maw, why dint you write me den? I be havin no idea. I cooda com home. Tiz evil dat you dint write me!' Mathew soon be realizin dat he be needin to hold back hiz anger. How cood he hav ev'r been reached? He be movin round a lot back den, and later too. Specialee, afta he be desertin frum da Fedral army. He dint be knowin wher he waz goin. He jest knowd he better be goin fast and far. Now feelin som shame, shood he be tellin hiz mother wot realy be happenin to him, or not? Stead, Mathew be stayin angry wit hur.

'So wots yur excuse Maw?'

I cood not write you. Matty, I dint know wher you waz. Somtimes, yur letters wood be returnin to me. I be ashamed dat I dint keep tryin. But to tell ya da truth, I be havin a vexin secret to tell ya. Afta a lengthy pause ... Matty, I caint read or write well. Ne'r cood. Long ago, my own paw alwayz be sayin I waz dumb and slow-minded. But yur fatha be knowin better and be savin me frum my family's shame. We both loved each otha very much.

He wood alwayz be protectin me frum dem otha folks too. Not ev'n you or Benny be knowin bout dis. So whence you be enlistin in da army up north, yur fatha wood writ in my words on som paper. Once dat letter waz done, I wood sign it and be havin it sent to you and Benny. Whence yur fatha died, I cood not be sendin ainy mor letters. I waz, and am, so ashamed dat I cood not read or write. Pleze be not hatin me.

Twas dis now da time fur Mathew to be reflectin and forgivin?

'Maw, I too be havin a burdensom secret. I cood not be receivin yur letters anyway cuz I waz no longer bein in da Union Army. So I cood not ev'r gittin'em dem. In '63, I waz a deserter.'

Mathew's motha be gaspin, but she dint be sayin anythin. She be knowin dat hur son need not now be hindered.

'Soon afta da war waz started, dem soldiers frum doze states north beginned to savage beat me, agin and agin. Dem officers wood be lookin de otha way, and wood tell me dat I be jest a copper-headed miscreant. Afta mor and mor whippins, I be decidin to escape dis torture. Som othas befor me had been tryin and failed. And most awl wer catched.

'Den afta a fast trial, dey wer sent to prison or wer executed. I be learnin frum dare mistakes. So I be stealin a horse, som guns, and be ridin east, fast. I better be shortin dis long story. I be endin up in Georgia and be joinin up wit a reb miltary unit dare. Afta dat, I be takin odd jobs capturin and returnin African contraband.'

Dis time, hiz maw did be interruptin hur son.

You did wot? Matty, befor you be continuin yur story, I jest want to tell ya bout som irony in wot you be sayin. You too wer once bein hunted down jest like you wer huntin down dem darkies. Dint yawl be understandin how doze darkies be feelin? Tiz zactlee like you be feelin. Dey too wer bein trapped and beatin. How I can forgiv yawl fur doin dat? I be knowin wots right and wrong. Do you? Yur fatha wood ne'r do dat. He wood alwayz be thinkin bout yur desertin da Union army. Specialee afta Benny waz kilt by dem secesh.

Dis waz now anotha time fur Mathew to be reflectin. He did so quietlee.

'Okay, maw, now dat you be puttin it dat way, I too be ashamed of my past thoughts and actions. Jest let me now be finishin my journey. Tiz a difcult one to tell yur own motha. Afta my darkie bounty huntin days, I be joinin up wit da 5th Georgia Cavalry til de war be endin. I waz den lookin fur a job. Ainy work wood be good den. Twas hard, but I be findin a job in Bama workin fur da Marion and Memphis Railroad. And I still do. Recent, I be gettin homesick and be needin som time to be clearin my head. So here I be. And no, I be not runnin frum doin anythin illegal.'

He be decidin not to tell hiz mother bout bein an aide-de-camp to dat railroad company prezdent, da former Confedrit genral, Nathan Forrest. Cuz of Mathew's work ethic, he waz soon in favor wit Genral Forrest. So much so, he be heppin da General to stablish da Ku Klux Klan, Mathew den be terrorizin dem freed darkies, Yankee carpetbaggers, and doze reconstructionists, awl infectin da south. Mathew waz much trusted fur hiz cavalry skills, and waz paid good.

Matty, I am so glad yur bein here now. Perhaps you can be heppin me a lil befor you be headin back to Georgia. Witout Benny and yur fatha here, tiz hard fur me to be keepin up wit awl dem ranchin chores. Bein alone out here be makin me much scared at times.

'How so, Maw? But furst, tell me mo bout yur readin and writin problems. Den, we can see how I can be heppin yawl.'

Matty, I aint bein able to read and write haz been much terrible fur me. It be like feelin yur a low-class person. Also, bein a woman, jest be makin it harder and harder. Tiz hard nuff bein a widow woman. Dat be makin me a target to awl doze men of ill will. But I do be havin som hope. Whence I waz recent in town, I be havin a chance chinwag wit a travelin doctor. I be tellin him bout dis readin problem I be havin awl my life.

And to my surprize, he be givin me somthin to be thinkin bout. Dat doctor be askin me many, many questions. Like (1) do ya be spellin words wrong by switchin da letters? (2) do ya be havin troubles focusin or listenin? (3) ar ya nervous bout talkin wit othas? And dare wer som otha questions dat I dint be knowin how to answer. awl my talkin waz yes sir or no sir. Den he be sayin I cood be havin back den dat same problem az Prezdent Jefferson be havin. Cain you imagin dat? Den, he be sayin dat dis problem be haz nothin to do wit not bein smart. Cain you imagin dat? So maybe you can be heppin me to be readin and writin bedder. Matty, pleze be thinkin bout dat.

'Maw, I be meanin to tell ya somthin else. I too be havin trouble readin and writin. I waz good at hidin my problem too. Perhaps, we can hep each otha. Togetter, we can be writin list of awl da things you be needin in town; and den we be goin to buy'em. Wot you think? We cood even hav lunch togetter and be practicin readin da menu.'

Sounds lika grand idea. I be startin to git ready. But know dat you be lookin so much like yur fatha whence he waz young; but ya must hav da workins of yur motha. And jest de opposite waz true fur Benny. Aint dat interestin? We cain talk bout dat lader.

Afta a wonerful day in town, Mathew be havin som troublesom thoughts and difcult decisions to be makin bout hiz futur. Do he be movin back home to Texas, or be stayin back in Georgia? If he be movin back to Texas, he cood den be re-inventin hizelf agin by becomin a rancher like hiz fatha. Den, he cood be heppin hiz motha save da ranch, and to hep hur wit da writin and readin. She cood be heppin him too.

Perhaps dat new Mathew cood later be a husband and a fatha hizelf. Or he cood simply be returnin to Georgia and be keepin hiz well-paid railroad job. And den also be makin good money by harassin doz freed darkies and othas exploitin da South. Dare, he could be a rich merchant.

But darez one big factor to be troublin Mathew. By hiz bein a Fedral Army deserter, he cain be a problem in both Texas and Georgia. Wher wood he be mor likelee to be found out? So now, Mathew belongs in Georgia, whilst Matty belongs in Texas. Who do he be wantin to be? Mathew or Matty? Okay, he need to be talkin to hiz maw fur som mor reflectin.

Mathew cood be stayin on a while at da ranch. He wood be feedin and mindin da stock, be buildin and mendin dem fences, and be choppin down trees fur da winter woodpile, and be fixin dat roof. Doze days wood soon be turnin inta weeks. Doze days do be flyin by fast. One day, Mathew be finalee visitin doze two headstones to be payin hiz respects to hiz Paw and Benny. Whilst dare, he be spotin anotha headstone, unmarked, and it be layin on da ground. He be wonderin why der be anotha gravestone. He wood ask.

'Well Maw, it be lookin like I be findin my way back to Georgia. Dare, I be needin to get som werk done. Oh, whence I be payin my respects to Pa and Benny, I den be seein anotha headstone. Who dat be fur?'

Matty, dat headstone be fur you. I be thinkin dat you n'er be writin me cuz yawl wer dead. Den you and Benny cain be togedder agin. But I alwayz hopin dat not be true. Or, if you be showin up afta I be dead, I be tellin da preacher to be usin dat headstone fur me instead.

'Well Maw, I still be alive and kickin. Den you can be keepin yur hopes high. I be hopin no decidin be needin to be done soon.'

No Matty, I be not wantin to be havin high hopes. I be wantin you to be comin home agin, and soon. O'er da years, I be learnin dat hope waz jest a lie to yurself.

Dare waz a uncomfortable silence. She be wantin hur boy back in Texas; and he be scared to be makin dat big decision now to be stayin or goin.

'Maw, I be enjoyin ar time togetter. But tiz time fur me to be goin. Do pleze gimme a big hug. Whence I be gettin back to Georgia, I den be finishin my duties, packin up my personals, buyin a buckboard wit som horses, and den be takin a month or so to git back to yawl.'

Or wood he be? Twas it realee dat easy to be lyin to hiz motha? She instinctivelee be knowin dat hur war-damaged son Matty truly missed bein loved; and dat hur sojourner son Mathew truly loved bein missed. Whooz futur wood prevail? Wer hiz war-time experiences too damagin to be gettin married to som unsuspectin Texas miss? Dat wood be much unkind. Den wood he be havin to reveal som of hiz many of wrong-doins?

Mathew be needin to be decidin who he realee be wantin to be on hiz long ride back to Georgia. But furst, he must be findin hiz Benny's true gravesite in Logan County, Arkansaw; and be havin a heart-to-hear conversation wit him. Afta all, dats wot brothas shood do. Only time wood be tellin if Mathew be stayin in Georgia, or it be Matty headin back home to Texas.

65. ON MEETING MYSELF
(A soldier hopes his war experiences will not foreshadow his future.)

```
Now dat dis horrific war tiz finalee o'er,
I be hopin to be meetin da person I am becomin.
Den togetter, a futur path we both be seekin.

On dis journey, will we, as one, become stronger?
Or will destiny be havin us to blindlee wander?
Now dat dis horrific war tiz finalee o'er.
```

66. CORNELIUS
(The author pays tribute to a Civil War era ancestor.)

My great-grandfather, Martin Gelock (1865-1959), died when I was twelve. He lived very near us in Grand Rapids, Michigan; and I spent many hours with him. We usually talked about books, and I also listened to him talk for hours about his interesting life. And especially his intriguing stories that his own father, my great-great-grandfather, Cornelius Gelock (1835-1915), told him.

Martin was an eager raconteur, and I was an avid listener. Because of that unique intergenerational bond, a powerful personal history was preserved. The two subjects that most enthralled me were Martin's adventures playing with American Indian boys across the Grand River, and his vivid recall of his father's life as a Union soldier in the Civil War.

Here is Cornelius' story:

Cornelius Gelock was born in 1835 in a small Dutch town. When he was young, his parents migrated to west Michigan, establishing a farmstead near Grand Rapids (GR). His father began working for a Dutch cartwright, and hoped young Cornelius would follow in his footsteps.

Cornelius' life was hard, but better than it was for many others at the time. At school, he learned to read, write and do arithmetic. At home, he learned how to ride a horse, shoot-straight a gun, build all things wooden, and drive his father's buckboard safely. He was never bored. The years passed, and Cornelius became an apprentice to being a wainwright.

By 1861, like all his friends and neighbors, he was reading the local *Herald* newspaper for news on Civil War battles. He learned about southern secessionists after they bombarded Fort Sumpter. He fretted about the Union forces being defeated at Bull Run, Ball's Bluff, and in many other places, not yet famous.

In December '61, Cornelius signed up for the Union Army. He enlisted in a GR muster, and was assigned to Company E. He became a 26-year-old gun battery Private in Michigan's First Regiment of its Light Artillery. Most of his boyhood friends had already mustered in September and November. He was soon a slow-moving train to Detroit, then onto Louisville for army training. He had ample time to think of what the future held.

All three GR volunteer companies (B, C & E) were sent west to join the Army of Ohio. In no time, they would be marching along the eastern side of the Mississippi River to join the siege of Corinth. Facing the intense fighting, and the deadly Yankee cannons, the battered Rebels finally surrendered.

Under the battlefield leadership of Generals Halleck and Grant, those Union volunteers stayed on mission. The three GR companies split up, and Cornelius' Company E marched east to Nashville. No longer a novice, he was now thick into the deadly bedlam of war.

To his surprise, it only took a week or so, in Tennessee, to turn the Rebel towns of Booneville and Nashville into Union blue. Company E marched northward into Kentucky to Perryville. In those three battles, Cornelius, like his comrades, witnessed 17,000 casualties, and he was often assigned to burial details. After little sleep, Company E was quick-marched westward back to the Mississippi River to join General Buell's campaign. No time to rest. Onwards.

General Grant would soon be fighting the cagey army of Albert Johnston. Company E, and thousands more of other Union soldiers, arrived just in time save the day. At Pittsburgh Landing, Shiloh was finally taken, after 23,000 boys were causalities. It was horrific to see the dead pile up before burial. Cornelius now knew how each day is a gift that can be taken at any time. One day your friend is alive, the next day he's dead. Tomorrow, him?

Mangled bodies, too many to count, need to be cared for. The surgeon's bloody saw takes off limb after limb after limb. The death toll was no longer shocking to newspaper readers from the eastern coast to the western plains. Cornelius often prayed with his comrades for just one more day of life.

Cornelius read about the Peninsular Campaign, and other battles, waiting for his next campaign assignment. His caisson driving and shooting skills were much improved, and never more needed. He learned to quick-load cannons and accurately aim the artillery shells.

Orders now came to be heading back east to take Nashville. Again. More coffins needed. Cornelius drove his laden caissons filled with munitions and grapeshot shells to the outskirts of the once-beautiful Nashville.

This fear and smell of death were everywhere. Death, the devil's own shadow, followed you around. After three months of fierce fighting, Nashville was retaken. Losing this city was a severe blow to the Confederate spirit.

In '62, the 22nd of September, Cornelius read about President Lincoln's *Emancipation Proclamation* to free some of those southern slaves. But only those from confederated States, not the others. This was wrong. Even so, the Federal Army now has two missions: to preserve the Union and to end the sin of slavery. There was no alternative for the volunteers of Company E but to fight on. Cornelius was fully committed to both objectives.

Company E pursued and fought those Rebs through the valleys and mountains. They also ambushed Confederate supply trains. The Union Army was finally winning back town after town, one by one by one. Many of the GR boys were now dead. Their Yankee lives eternally hushed, their families broken.

Then it happened, in Chatanooga! An enemy shell exploded Cornelius' caisson through its vulnerable spoked wheels. He was badly injured. But so many others were killed all around him. Why not him?

Cornelius survived, but barely. His war was over. He had served twenty-three, long, harsh months on the frontlines. Now, it was history. The long, slow train ride back to Grand Rapids, through Louisville and Detroit, was surreal. Going over every bump on the track intensified his pain. He had lots of time to think. To think about his comrades, dead, badly wounded, or barely alive. And himself. Could he still work? In his former trade? If not, then what? Even though he was one of the lucky ones, would he be healing quickly, slowly, or not at all??

He was not just concerned about his body healing, but his mind too was wounded. It seemed to play tricks on him. His sleep was fitful and his dreams terrifying.

Finally, back home, Cornelius' body took much longer to heal than the doctors expected or than he had hopefully imagined. He had a lot more time to think and to read the local Herald again. He followed Company E, especially, as they went into battle at Chattanooga, Atlanta and The March to the Sea. The GR boys of Company B were also in the battles for Atlanta and the March to the Sea, before heading north to the Carolinas' Campaign. And Company C, after Atlanta, chased Hood's rebel army westward. The hunt for victory was relentless.

While the Rebs killed many GR boys, many more fell victim to deadly swamp diseases. No matter the price for victory, the surviving volunteers of Michigan's First Regiment of Light Artillery never lost their resolve to win the war.

After the war, Cornelius was haunted by his having survived while so many comrades had perished. Why was he still alive? Why hime? God's Will? Luck? A punishment?

Survivor guilt became his burden as it was for thousands of those who are spared in battle, but are condemned to see again and again the faces of dead comrades. A guilt difficult to endure. And to be seen with suspicion by the mothers and wives of fallen friends and neighbors. Why did you come home, and they did not?

Cornelius carried mixed feelings about his caisson being destroyed and he only being injured, while so many others died. He feared becoming an outcast by his fellow volunteers. Battle can be so unfair. No one truly knows when their time is up. It can be like a roll of the dice. Just trying to avoid old 'snake eyes.'

Cornelius knew he had performed his duties well, but so did those other brave soldiers. He feared becoming emotionally dead under the weight of his burden of survival. For some, living was a greater curse than dying. Yet, he was very much surprised and relieved that the people in Grand Rapids showed no animosity toward him. Especially the veterans. But his calmness by day gave way to his nightly terrors. It would take time.

In the years to come, Cornelius made a good life for himself and others. He became his own boss and was widely acknowledged as an expert wainwright. He hired as many veterans as he could and built sturdier wagons, with more dependable spoked wheels. Getting married and becoming a father speeded up his recovery.

His recovery was enhanced by becoming a devoted husband and a doting father to his first new-born son, Martin. He hoped Martin would also become an expert wainwright and be expanding his business. And in time, that wish became a reality. Martin, embodied hope, joy, and the future. Cornelius dreamed of Martin becoming a wainwright and of expanding the family business came true.

Though now owned by another, the business lives on in 2024 as the Gelock Transfer Line, in Grand Rapids – providing heavy machinery and moving services throughout Michigan. And when Martin Gelock died, he bequeathed his father's Civil War service medal to his great-grandson, Drew Albritten.

67. TO LOVE AGAIN

Befor dis war, I be knowin I waz much loved by othas.
Afta da war, twas much nummed by da deaths of brothas.
Now I be fightin off my demons wit som hepp frum anotha.
And I be prayin to agin be a lovin husband, fatha and brotha.

68. I, SOLDIER
(Inspired by conversations with WW2 Medal of Honor recipient Lt Col Matt Urban.)

In war, ev'ry soldier be stowin awl hiz pain and fears aside.
And be carryin 'Ole Glory' forward wit unwaverin pride.
Dis flag be givin us courage whence dare militaries collide.

At reunions, comrades still be keepin dark feelins inside.
And be wonderin why dey lived whilst so many othas died.
Ev'n many be hav doz evenin terrors dat ar hard to hide.

Mainy soldiers be thinkin dat feelins waz a sign of weakness.
So whence dey die, we awl be sayin 'dis man twaz a good soldier.'
So whence I die, I be hopin dey be sayin da same, mo or less.
I be thinkin', I'd radder be a better man now dan jest a good soldier.

Epilogue:
Picket and Potato-Peeler

(Some backstory experiences of a Civil War reenactor.)

It was a hot and sticky Virginia day in 1981, when I first explored Alexandria's Oldtown. In my meanderings, I found a unique antique bookstore just a few blocks up from the Potomac River. In this unexpectedly well-dusted book shop was full array of old Americana publications and vintage memorabilia. I was looking for something special for my father's upcoming August birthday, less than a month away. In addition to having a plethora of second-hand books for sale, there was to my surprise a large collection of pre-owned baseball cards hidden in the back of this librarian's paradise.

Growing up, my favorite baseball team was the heartbreaking Detroit Tigers. While slowly perusing through those player cards, it brought back many wonderful family memories. I recalled my father telling me about his Akron boyhood friend who had become a successful Major League baseball player, Gene Woodling. While methodically rifling through those other older cards, I found Gene's Topps card, an outfielder for the New York Yankees. Although he was over-shadowed by two future Hall of Famers, Joe DiMaggio and Mickey Mantle, this player's card would be the perfect gift.

While waiting at the congested check-out counter, preparing to pay for this over-priced 1952 Topps baseball card for my father as well as for an under-priced early edition of *Uncle Tom's Cabin* for myself, I spotted a reproduction of a former Union Army recruitment poster. On it was an invitation to join a local Civil War reenactors' group. Their meeting was to be held this coming Saturday in a café in Oldtown, near the historic Marshall House. I already knew that at the beginning of the Civil War, in May of 1861, Colonel Elmer Ellsworth had been killed there trying to take down its seditionist Confederate flag. I had long been interested in American history, in general, and in its Civil War, in particular. My interest in history began when listening to stories told to me by my great grandfather, Martin Gelock (1865-1959); my grandfather, Carl Coulier (1896-1969); and my World War II veteran father, William Allbritten (1922-2004).

Having recently moved from Michigan just a few months before starting my new job in Washington, D.C. (statutorily named the "Douglass Commonwealth," after the well-known abolitionist and author, Frederick Douglass), I thought to visit the Marshall House prior to attending the reenactors' meeting. After that interesting visit, while at the café, I chatted with several of the local group members. One friendly, but earnest, gray-templed man approached me saying, "I am the officer of this fine Union Army regiment and would look forward to you becoming our newest 'picket and potato-peeler.' And if you are committed, I will even throw in an extra onion or two." A living history event was scheduled for the following weekend; and I signed up to attend. Being new to the D.C. area, I thought this could be a good opportunity to meet new people with some similar interests. And so began my two decades as a Civil War reenactor. I was initially known as a "pie-eater" or "fresh fish," just as all the other new Union Army recruits.

My Company of reenactors was fully committed to factually honoring our nation's history; and I took this responsibility seriously. When taking part in numerous living history events, I made every effort to accurately perform my new duties. Every reenactor was fully immersed in learning the history of its own Union Company, in their movements throughout the Civil War, and of the soldiers' typical experiences. And I faithfully did so as well.

At the living history events, from the many different sutlers hawking their variety of goods, I eagerly purchased a replica wool Union uniform. I also bought period reproduction weaponry, tinware, cutlery, haversack, kepi, and many other military accoutrements. This would become a costly past-time, but within reason.

Those bulky blue uniforms were not made to fit you very well, and those leather boots were a large one-size-fits-all. Additional socks would be needed. Interestingly, both the left and right boots also had the same specifications. Why? I came to find the macabre truth of this feature. If a soldier lost a boot in combat, or elsewhere, the same sized boot made it much easier to replace. After all, dead soldiers don't need their boots anymore. Also in battle, many soldiers could easily lose their kepis, buttons, or other regalia. And to replace them then, the Union Army would deduct the cost of those specific items from their meagre monthly pay. So, after a battle, some surviving soldiers could be seen scavenging certain items off their fallen comrades for their own future use, or for sale to other comrades at a price much lower than would have been deducted by the regiment's Quartermaster. At first, this reality was hard to imagine.

I had joined this regular Army group portraying a midwestern Private who was a semi-literate soldier in Company C, 2nd Regiment, II Corps of the Army of the Potomac. We would all train and drill as the soldiers did back then, learning all their military maneuvers and the historical timelines. Later, I would buy a well-kept original Amoskeag Springfield rifle with its accompanying rusty bayonet. My company comrades were amazed at the fine condition this rifle was in, and that it still fired well. I would only use this special rifle at living history events; but had another well-used replica for the battle reenactments.

Over my reenacting years, with my over-stuffed haversack and heavy carpetbag, I took part in over twenty-five battle scenarios and in numerous scores of living history events. As a regular Army Private, I was expected to regularly wash and clean my uniform and other regalia, to scrub my tinware and cutlery, to polish my weapons, to shine my boots and clean my leather goods. I was also expected to routinely picket-watch, prepare meals on kitchen duty, feed and wash the horses, and to gather wood for the nightly campfires. I soon learned how to quickly pitch and dismantle my small half-tent, and to flawlessly pitch and dismantle the larger officer tents. The watching officers would often critique my every move.

Being a lowly Private, I also did more than my fair share of potato-peeling; and in the evenings, would stand watch most of the nights impatiently waiting for the next detail to take my place. Did there really need to be a watchful picket? Being a night picket was much like being a security guard at a local shopping mall. But there were a few times when some local hooligans would sneak into camp to do their late-night pillaging. If caught, we would place them over night into a deep underground dirt jail being covered by its heavy, iron latticework. After some time in this dank and bug-filled pit, such pillaging would soon end. It was no longer fun for those incorrigibles when caught. We took this pillaging seriously; but harmlessly handled it. Later, there would be much fewer nightly incursions.

Once my daily chores were completed, I would read old books and newspapers as well as any periodicals of this dreadful Civil War era. In my personal pursuit for authenticity, I only read books which were published before the 1860s, such as *Uncle Tom's Cabin*, *On Walden Pond*, *The Scarlet letter*, *The Tale of Two Cities*, and *The Narrative of Sojourner Truth* as well as some Edgar Allan Poe books. I would acquire them from my newly found and friendly Alexandria antique bookstore, and would often enjoy a loyalty discount. Reading those old *Philadelphia Inquirers* and *New York Times* newspapers as well as the illustrated issues of *Harper's Weekly* magazine, could make those long nights of bivouacking seem to pass by more quickly. I would also read them when not reenacting. A pleasant change of pace to my typical paperwork.

During any daytime down-time, I could often be seen reading and writing. My half-tent mate was a Corporal, and he soon became my patient mentor. As a joke, he would frequently call me, "Bookworm." Then, my Sargent began to simply call me, "Worm." And soon thereafter, my Regimental Lieutenant, whom I first meet at the Alexandria recruitment meeting, now just called me, "Private Worm." And that name stuck. Most all my fellow reenactors would never know my real name. Nicknames were an important part of a reenactor's persona. At first, I was a bit miffed; but later reframed this moniker as the term of endearment. In time, I became "Private Worm, the Storyteller."

At night, sleeping rough was always tough, no matter how hot or cold the evening. My half-tent Corporal would always grumble about most everything, but especially about the stony and uneven terrain beneath our tent. After all, we were indeed reenacting a time of this great war when real Union soldiers were always drilling and marching, getting used to the mud and bugs, handling the intense heat or extreme cold, and when boredom could only be overcome by their fear of death or a losing a limb. Our reenacting was never advertised as Club Med; and as a reenactor, you could leave at any time. The actual Civil War soldier could not. Then, "leaving" was called "cowardice" or "desertion" or "A.W.O.L." Unlike those real soldiers, we were only acting at trying to be realistic, or being sick, wounded or dead.

Oftentimes, we had to move and re-pitch our tent after a long day of marching drills and other daily duties. In doing so, practicing speed and precision were important. To be in character, I also needed to learn the ins and outs of each tedious task, and to unfortunately experience the feelings of exhaustion and discomfort. In one discomforting instance, I needed to buy a set of Civil War period prescription spectacles, and to never again to wear my modern ones during any reenactment. While these new spectacles were savage to wear, it was still better than to be marching or drilling blindly. To heal my lacerated nose, a beekeeper comrade suggested I buy honey and apply it liberally. That worked for the most part, except when it attracted bees and other insects. At least, this honey could also be a welcomed supplement my hardtack, bread and stew. Honestly, this honey was also good for many other things as well, including relieving my relentless thirst during a long reenactment whenever my canteen water was gone.

Going to-and-from our scheduled events was often comical. Usually, when clumsily getting into and out of a car in full regalia, especially with a rifle or sword in tow. Any onlookers would frequently smile or look quizzically as I clanked and stumbled about in my once-new Union gear. But at times, it was less amusing. When traveling to events into the South, it could be awkward at best, and sometimes just plain scary. It's hard to imagine how some Union reenactors nowadays would be welcomed in our hyper-polarized country when authentically participating in a living history event in Dixie.

Once staying at a quintessential roadside southern motel, I was proudly wearing my Union blue at its recommended diner, and soon encountered several insults and obscenities from a pathetic few: "Damn you Yankee boy!' and 'You blue-bellied scallywag," or even much worse. You learned to just shrug off such insults. But sometimes, I would retort too loudly by calling those pathetic few, "slubberdegullion scallywags" or "rapscallion miscreants." Some would inquisitively ask me what I had meant, and I would simply tell them, "Go look it up." These days, one could probably get assaulted for such a simple retort.

In reenacting a battlefield scenario, if you were designated to "die" or to be "wounded," and were just lying there motionless on the ground just playing your historical part, a Rebel reenactor might just heartlessly kick you in the ribs or stomp on your fingers. Sometimes they would lean down and whisper, "Lee surrendered, but I didn't." Very soon, you learned how to safely curl up and keep your face covered to avoid any dirt or stones being kicked your way. Sad, but true. A few of these Rebels would proudly call these reenactments as their "Lost Cause" revenge; and proceed to call us "Darkie Lovers" or "Low Life Carpetbaggers" or even more graphic epithets. But definitely not the vast majority. Yet a few Confederate reenactors just wanted to rewrite history to further glorify the "Southern War Against Yankee Aggression." That was then; but now is this alarming mantra on the rise again?

In time, I was finally accepted into the old-timers group. My passionate commitment for detail had paid off. For some events, I would bring my original rustic 1860's-period portable stove. It could simultaneously boil up to four large pots of coffee when placed precisely over a raging campfire. My Federal Army cronies would then drink that hot, strong, and dreadful coffee while chin-wagging about home or this war in an 1860's manner. Soon enough, other reenactors joined us as we badly sang period songs, awkwardly danced around the campfire, and had joyfully guzzled down a few too many hard spirits.

Periodically, I would attend what seemed to be a revival of Stephen Foster's greatest hits from the 1850s and before. It was quite enjoyable. During reenactments, our singing of any songs from the 1860s could become complicated. We were not allowed to sing any songs written after the time of any specific reenactment event. For example, no 1863 (or later) song could be sung during an 1862 (or earlier) event. One Company reenactor would be unofficially designed to know the exact publishing dates of all such songs. I am glad it wasn't me.

When I wasn't reading at night, or on picket watch, or just struggling to sleep, I began writing my ideas for poems and short stories. They were usually steeped in the themes, language, and the feelings about this War. At first, my writings were much influenced by Stephen Foster's many rhyming couplet parlor ballads. Later, I ventured into capturing unusual historical facts or miscellaneous reflections I had heard during the evening campfire conversations. In time, I was asked to read some of my earlier poetry and stories. I was embarrassed at first.

I had been keeping a diary of my thoughts of what a typical Civil War soldier might be thinking about ... his emotions, fears, tensions, and friendships. And to do so in their own vernacular and accent. It was my intention to have these writings capture the language and modes of expression of the 1860s, as we had come to now know them from past literature, rare recordings, oral histories, and the like. Thus, I became the Company's unofficial storyteller. My diary was sadly lost later; but my jotted notes and memory served me well.

During these reenactments, I always tried to stay in my character's semi-literate voice; and got used to being mocked by some. Yet, several of my other comrades, then called "possums," enjoyed my portrayals and storytelling. Unexpectedly, a few were even brought to tears. Some would later give me suggestions on topics to write or talk about; and a few would anonymously slide their written ideas under my tent flap.

Word spread. I was more often asked to read some of my history-based writings during living history events. Then later, to a few organizations and schools on certain special occasions. I usually attended those events in full Union regalia. I was surprised, and still am upon reflection, that most people have little knowledge about the American Civil War and its ramifications for today's world. Yet, I felt empowered to share my 1860's writings; and through them, my thoughts and beliefs about this terrible time in the nation's history. Which for some, it appears that this regrettable Civil War is not yet over.

I was empowered to continue my poetry readings and storytelling, but at times there existed a credible risk. At one of those reenactor impromptu fireside concerts during the Ball's Bluff reenactment (also known as the Battle of Leesburg), after one reading, a revived regional dispute got out of hand. One rowdy, rabble-rouser took a harmless verbal squabble and turned it into a bruising kerfuffle. Following an amateurish brawl between some Union and Confederate reenactors, I, along with few other Company comrades, we were placed into a make-shift jail. It was called the "sunken calaboose." Early that following cold morning, although being quite smelly and dirty, we chagrined pugilists were ordered to prepare a grits-based breakfast for hundreds of hungry (and innocent) reenactors. We deservedly ate the cold and sloppy leftovers; and learned a powerful lesson about how hard it was for some reenactors to separate their living history responsibilities from their enduring current grievances. I would apologize for my lack of judgement.

During another living history event, celebrating President Lincoln's 1862 *Emancipation Proclamation*, many reenactors from both sides debated upon which Civil War battles were the most important Union or Confederate victories. I was not surprised that our Yankee boys' choice was Gettysburg with the Battle of Antietam Creek (a.k.a., Sharpsburg) and Pittsburgh Landing (a.k.a., the Battle of Shiloh) being close seconds. And I was not surprised that the Rebel boys' choice was Chancellorsville with the battles of Fredericksburg and First Manassas (a.k.a., First Bull Run) being close seconds. Others may disagree. I did. For instance, I thought the Siege of Vicksburg had more military significance than the Battle of Antietam Creek. Anyway, historians will have their opinions, as well as you.

Then, a showstopper occurred when a well-intoxicated Rebel shouted out that the greatest and most important victory in the Civil War took place at Fort Pillow (Henning, Tennessee). What? Wasn't that the battle where hundreds of surrendering and unarmed colored soldiers, who fought for the Union, were brutally massacred under the command of the

Confederate General Nathan Bedford Forrest? (Wasn't he the same N.B. Forrest who was the first Grand Wizard of the original Ku Klux Klan? Yes!). I was dumbstruck, as were most others. This sort of proud, blatant, and outspoken racism was new to me. Even though I had before lived in a diverse community and represented its multi-cultural district in the Michigan Legislature, I was not fully aware of the unapologetic excesses of this current, deep, dark, abrasive, and ugly side of American life.

It became quite clear to me that you need not scratch the surface too much to bring out the intense racism and hatred of some reenactors. Tragically, the racial abuse of African Americans (then, simply known as "slaves" or "Africans" or "darkies") continues to this day, to our nation's continuous shame. To me, these living history events became even more important and meaningful than I had ever previously thought. This in-your-face racism helped me to further shape and focus my values, views, career choices, and my proactive commitment to making a positive difference for all in any way I could. This journey continues.

On the lighter side, even during the Civil War there were some extensive down-times. This led a few soldiers to create some well-meaning, comrade-directed chaos. Besides handling my daily duties, I too enjoyed springing pranks and playing poker. But I did draw the line when such pranks would ever veer into the personal or harmful. Some others would have no such lines. To spring pranks or general tomfoolery on comrades was commonplace, then as well as now, even though that prankster could be subject to some disciplinary action, if caught. You had to be fully trustful of your partners-in-crime to avoid being snitched upon. To be honest, I did enjoy a good prank, even if I became its target. And at times, Private Worm was.

Most of these pranks tended to mirror those of the 1860s. Always a favorite, was to loosen a victim's tent stakes, block the tent entrance with all things noisy, and then cause a commotion outside. When the unsuspecting victim would quickly exit the tent, he would trip over those things noisy; and the tent would collapse behind him. Then, from every direction, came the huzzahs, cheers, and laughter. If the victim as a good sport, we would help him re-pitch his tent. Other pranksters would hide a comrade's boots or rifle just before the morning reveille and then watch the ensuing chaos. Pranks also included hiding one's blanket on a cold night, or placing smelly horse poo under one's tent, or adding bugs to one's meal. Upon reflection, did this childish tomfoolery perhaps help soldiers, in some weird way, to stay nobly connected to one another? Some would agree.

However, cheating at cards was never ever tolerated. When those poker-players were caught, and that would usually happen, the cheater would be irreverently placed into an iron-covered pit for the duration of a living history event. A repeat offender could be banished from the privilege to reenact. Back in the day, soldiers could be dishonorably discharged, lose their stripes, or be put in prison. Looks like there were grifters at every time in American history.

More on the lighter side, I enjoyed reading David Ross Locke's humorous letters of the 1860s. He used the pseudonym of "Petroleum Vesuvius Nasby," or just "Nasby", to portray a drunken, braggart Copperhead who was always in trouble. Then, as now, Locke's writings are a fun and informative read. Even President Lincoln wrote about his enjoying Nasby's many misadventures.

During the reenactment of the 2nd Battle of Bull Run (a.k.a., 2nd Battle of Manassas), my Company officer decided to set up a field hospital simulation for those attending. To do so, we spotted and retrofitted a dilapidated wooden shed, and nine of us volunteered to participate. Our Company officer was the moderator, our Sargent was the surgeon, two Corporals were the wounded soldiers, and four Privates (which included me) were the battlefield litter bearers, and a reenactor's wife was the nurse. And she really was one. The moderator began by explaining to the audience the historical importance of the Sanitation Corps and how it helped wounded soldiers during and after battles. The surgeon then, while holding a "bloody" saw (with its thick red paint dripping), described graphically what the usual medical practices were at that time in history when receiving the wounded. That's when we four litter bearers showed up carrying our two wounded soldiers. The nurse directed the litter bearers to bring those two wounded into our make-shift field hospital.

The shed door was immediately closed by the surgeon when he entered the field hospital. A moment later, the howling and screaming would begin by us privates. Red paint would be poured over the two wounded soldiers, the surgeon, and the nurse. The surgeon had a wood log in which he would begin to loudly saw inside the shed. As the howling continued, the nurse would throw some newly painted prosthetic limbs out the windows for all the attendees to see. Some attendees would scream and squeal; but still watched. A few left. Soon, two litter bearers would carry out one once-wounded, and now dead, soldier out of the hospital and take him behind the shed. The bearers would return on the double-quick with only their empty litter and its bloody sheet that once covered the soldier. The surgeon soon came out to tell the audience that one soldier may still survive the operation. He went on to explain how difficult it was in battle to continually be moving the operating tables from window to window because the limps were piling up too high outside. After some silence, the moderator stepped forward to answer any questions or respond to any comments of the attendees. After addressing those, to our astonishment, there was some appreciative applause.

The "good word" on our simulation got around fast, and we all felt some pride in a job well done. We held two more events that day, with each having a much greater audience. We were now receiving many more loud "huzzahs" and "hoorahs." It was quite emotional for all. Yet, our simulation was too much for a few to bear. The reality of war is horrifying, more than we could have ever demonstrated properly. But we performed it well enough.

That evening, following the field hospital simulation and before *Taps*, I went A.W.O.L. There was a fundraising event I attended annually that provided its proceeds to a local domestic abuse program. They always appreciated my frequent donations. It was hosted by some of my Kentuckian friends who named it, "A Taste of the South." The sponsors usually wore antebellum garb, and the attendees were told to dress casually. To add some sparkle to this event, I did not change my clothes and attended in my full Union regalia. After some gasps and muttering, it was an enjoyable and relaxing evening picnic with a potluck buffet of assorted food specialties from all the southern states. I especially liked the juicy slab of North Carolina barbequed pork ribs basted in a thick bourbon sauce along with a large slice of Georgia sweet potato pie with a double-dollop of cream. Too soon, it was time to go, and to sneak back undetected into the Union encampment.

When entering my area of the encampment, I was accosted by a most diligent Yankee picket who politely asked me for the password. When leaving earlier, I had forgotten to find out what the password would be for this night. This picket gave me two options: 1) to stay out all night with him and to being tied to a nearby fence post; or 2) to be placed into an underground pit that served as a jail cell. Been there, done that. So, I decided on a different option, to just sleep in my car. Early that next morning, I was startled by a bugler's ear-piercing reveille. And to my surprise, I re-entered the Union encampment uninterrupted; and washed up some knowing it would become a long, long, long day.

A week or so later, my commanding officer had received an official letter from an attorney to cease-and-desist from all future field hospital simulations. One of the attendees, who had fainted, filed a complaint. Fearing a lawsuit, and any other potential impending litigation, our organizational higher-ups declared that our field hospital simulations were perhaps too graphic for some. We would no longer be able to present this kind of battlefield scenario in the future. It was a shame that we could not reach a "win-win" compromise.

In the reenactment of the Battle of Antietam Creek (a.k.a., Sharpsburg), it was my responsibility was to be shot and killed three times. This would become a long and arduous day. The heat was taking its toll on everyone. So, how does a reenactor get picked to "die" three times? Before each battle, our Company's Lieutenant would meet with us and bring his "bag of death." This small burlap bag contained marbles of three colors – white, red, and black ones. Since historical records indicate how many soldiers died or were wounded in any battle, or in a any part of that battle, these colored marbles would be determined in the same ratio. A "black marble" meant you were killed in action, a 'red marble' meant you were wounded, and a 'white marble' meant you luckily survived. In this reenactment, I would select one marble for each of the three parts of the battle to be reenacted that one dreadful day in American history - for the bridge, the woods, and the cornfield.

Here's what happened. When it was my turn to reached into that "bag of death," I was gobsmacked. For the Stone Bridge engagement, I selected a black marble; for the West Woods engagement, I again selected a black marble; and for The Cornfield's engagement, I once more selected a black marble. What are the odds of that happening? Quite surreally, I could then choose when, how, and where to "die" in each of those three engagements.

At the bridge, I cleverly decided to die immediately by the side of the road, just before the creek. Then, I would be able to watch what would be happening ahead; as well as to avoid getting trampled by my comrades-in-arms. During that engagement, several reenactors, on or after the bridge, ended up with broken fingers or arms as well as earning multiple bruises. In the dense woods, lumbering up a quite steep and slippery incline was extremely exhausting for me. However, playing dead there, in the shade, was a blessed reward. Yet, my death in the now-trampled cornfield was by far the worst of the engagements, both mentally and physically. Wanting to see all what was transpiring, I was determined to "die" leaning up against a split-rail fence. There was no shade there or anywhere else close by. My Company had been reenacting all day long in the dreaded heat. My woollen uniform dripped with sweat, and my canteen and honey pot were both empty. Now what?

At this point, a strange reality set in. I realized I was living out in some measure what those Union soldiers had to endure in heat of that September in 1862, soon to be known as deadliest day in Civil War history. Yet those Antietam survivors still when on to fight day in and day out to save the Union. They risked their lives so others might live. By contrast, at the end of this reenactment day, I would be able to get into my air-conditioned car and drive home to a comfy house. The carnage then was ghastly, and we painstakingly tried to represent what history had recorded.

My musings ended abruptly as I felt two Confederate rifles being strategically placed on each shoulder. I was being used as a sighting aid. They fired, reloaded, and fired again and again. The gun smoke powder burnt my eyes, filled my nose, and clogged my throat. Within seconds, I had lost my hearing. It took several days to get it back, but my headaches lasted longer. If it was 1862, I would not have had this problem since I would have already been dead. But today, I certainly learned the value of discreetly wearing earplugs. The veteran reenactors already knew this; but apparently, I had missed that briefing. The sutlers did not sell earplugs since it would have been historically inappropriate. But they directed me to a nearby pharmacy that did have them in stock. Those earplugs would be most suitable for any future battle reenactments.

Looking back to that split-rail fence situation, without turning my head too much, I could clearly visualize what the Cornfield would have looked like 120 years before. The battleground then was littered with Union blue uniforms. Survivor testimonials of that terrible day indicated that a soldier could walk across that field without even touching the ground; and now, the reenactors did the same. For hours and hours, those with red marbles would scream and cry out, and those with black marbles just laid there motionless for hours. It brought tears to my eyes and a deep sorrow.

The visitors, who came to witness those reenactments, usually had no idea how loud the blasting sounds would be, how smelly the rancid odors would be, and how thick the fog-like smoke would be. Those sounds, smells and smoke were as real now as it was back then. Except, the major difference was that no bullets or cannon shells were being fired.

My appalling headache and hearing issues prevented me from participating in the after-battle events and celebrations. While disappointed, I knew that my efforts, and the efforts of those other North and South reenactors, again honored those many who died on this forsaken battlefield at Antietam Creek.

Later that day, at home, an intense wave of shame washed over me. Followed by another wave of deep appreciation for those who risked their lives for a worthy cause. Not only did all those soldiers pay a high price, but so did their families, friends, and neighbors as well as the urban or rural communities where they lived.

Reenacting the Battle of Gettysburg, on its 125th anniversary, was the peak experience for me. After week of never-ending days and nights, I had another glimpse into the reality of the 1860's soldier. It was gruelling. I had learned so much about the importance of this battle in American history, its lost humanity, and the futility of war. It had pivotal importance that would forever change the course of history for generations to come. You cannot look back on a field full of fallen bodies and not be horrified. Not to mention its immense collateral damage for the nearby non-combatants.

Before Gettysburg, I had already bizarrely learned how to properly "die" or be "wounded" during a battle scenario. This is important because there was usually an intelligent audience watching this event. Some of those in attendance were recognized historians, Civil War history experts, self-taught history buffs, and former reenactors. You had to always be authentic 24/7. You also learned where, how and when to die or be wounded, preferably in the shade. But shade can still be quite burdensome while lying motionless on the ground, hour after hour after hour. You had to plan well-enough ahead, and knowing the weather forecast for that day could be useful. All was going well in Gettysburg until the last day of this 3-day battle reenactment, when …

After days of drawing the white marble, I had finally picked a black one initial engagement on that last day of combat. During that earlier skirmish, I had been laying "dead" for hours, and had again too soon emptied my canteen and honey jar. Poor planning on my part. But now, I had to answer nature's call. How do I break the sacred code that dead soldiers don't move? Do I just befoul my woollen trousers? No way. I simply pretended I really drew a red marble instead for that engagement and would slowly crawl over to the nearby grove of trees to relieve myself. Not so simple. While it was just a short distance, it soon became a complicated crawl having to go around or over other reenactors. Since I had to move more rapidly into that dense thicket, I decided to use my trusty Springfield rifle as a crutch to prop myself up. Then, in a timelier manner, I dragged myself over to that nearby shady copse of trees. That's when answering nature's call in this concealed thicket, I heard a thunderous voice from on high, "Cut, dammit!"

Up in the trees was a two-man team of Ted Turner's sizeable film crew who were now hiding in what looked like a highly perched, camouflaged hunter's blind. Those two had been capturing this part of the battle, including what was supposed to be "my dying moment." The consequential upshot of my down shot was that my potential movie career had come to a brief and tragic end after eventually answering nature's call. I was gratefully edited out of the final version of the four-hour movie, *Gettysburg*. Oh well! At least I was finally able to "die" in peace in the shade.

Later, just before Picket's Charge, I had returned to my Company, but was then re-assigned to a different battle unit of soldiers from the Midwest. Our collective duty was to protect the long line of General Meade's artillery. We were all ordered to lay on the ground in two single-lined ranks with our rifles aiming toward the frontlines. When the Union cannons were ordered to demolish Picket's charging men, each cannon volley would lift us off the ground. The frequent booming concussions were intensely terrifying. Once again, it was like watching a silent movie in a smoke-filled room. And once again, I could smell and taste the cannon powder. But this time, I was wearing my new modern earplugs. Which meant I could not hear any drummed or bugled orders. But at least, I would be able to hear afterwards. In short, drawing a white marble did not necessary mean it would be easy going.

My memory of those all-consuming sensations at the Battle of Gettysburg stayed with me for years to come. After Picket's Charge, I was reunited with my brethren from Company C. After a well-earned rest and gulping down some water, we slowly marched in 4s back to our bivouac area to take down our tents. Except for us privates, we were ordered to completely clean up the encampment area. By evening, I was utterly exhausted and hungry. Even the cold grits and stew would be a treat. Next, came my quiet time to reflect upon my day's experiences; and to perhaps sleep well.

For me, it was important to write down my thoughts and feelings post-haste as I had done each evening before. If not done soon, I could easily forget some of those mind-numbing details. The next morning, I leisurely packed up my gear and left the motel contented and reflective. We had all once again played our parts well in keeping this tragic history alive and factual. But whatever had happened to those soldiers who survived? It became even more important for me to imagine the true impact the Civil War had not only on a soldier's wartime experiences, but also what happened in their post-war life. I started writing.

Driving home seemed out of context, yet spiritual. I did not turn the car radio on. I slept well later. For tomorrow, it was going to be truly weird experience returning to work. Much work needed to be done after my week-long absence. Again, it was sometimes difficult to give my full attention to my real-life obligations. My thoughts would often drift back to those soldiers in blue who fought to save the Union.

As I later watched the movie Gettysburg, it was greatly satisfying to verify the commitment made by the thousands upon thousands of the reenactors who participated in the background, without any pay and without any proper acknowledgement. All do their reenacting from their hearts to ensure this history would not be forgotten, concealed, or distorted. Also, as in the filming of the movie *Glory*, many of my fellow reenactors, North and South, brought forth their authenticity to the set; and kept the production costs down on an otherwise prohibitive filming budget. Glory was successful, with Denzel Washington receiving an Academy Award for Best Supporting Actor. Huzzah!

For the record, not everyone appreciated our dedication and efforts. A day or so after the reenactment of this Battle of Gettysburg, I received a surprising phone call from my Commanding Officer. He said that some of our Company C comrades, and scores of many other reenactors from different Union and Confederate units, had unexpectedly received citations for violating some regulations of the Gettysburg National Cemetery grounds. The National Park Service (NPS) does forbid the carrying of any rifles, pistols, swords, bayonets, and any other dangerous weapons on any of their sacred sites. But for such reenactments, those regulations were typically waived. Not this time. Thus, many reenactors had incurred heavy fines from over-zealous NPS Rangers. How stupid was this! Reenactments bring positive attention to NPS national cemeteries, and as a result more people would visit them. It's simple, the more people who visit, the more sizable the revenue, and the greater opportunity to maintain or improve NPS services and properties. Such short-sightedness.

Only a select knew of Private Worm's real day job as a U.S. Presidential Appointee. This meant I had some access to certain high-level contacts within the U.S. Department of Interior's (USDOI) Office of the Secretary. I soon scheduled an unofficial meeting to discuss the citation issue with both USDOI and NPS officials. They were somewhat confused and hesitant on how to properly proceed in remedying this citation problem. I simply told them to resolve this matter now or be prepared to deal with the media soon. They were generally insulted by my threat, and the meeting ended abruptly. Yet, my insider USDOI contact quietly informed them that I do not bluff. A long story shorter, as a result, no further citations were issued, and no fines were to be collected. And for any future reenactment activities held on NPS properties, the participating units would again receive waivers for their regalia and weaponry. Huzzah!

During my time as a reenactor, I would frequently have some critical work obligations to complete. At those times, I would go A.W.O.L., and my half-tent partner would cover for me. If a task or function was to be held close to Washington, D.C., I could quickly change into my work clothes that I kept in the trunk of my car, and soon head off. If not close to an event, and there was no way to get back in a timely manner, I would find a nearby hotel, motel, restaurant, or Waffle House where I could read, analyze, write, or make calls. I was usually working on some policy papers, draft speeches, or Congressional reports. Also, at night, my Corporal mentor would sometimes catch me writing draft reports with a flashlight while hiding underneath my blanket. He would friendly remind me to only be reading pre-1860s books by candlelight. Unfortunately, Private Worm, also had some other understandable obligations that needed to be attended to, like several of the other reenactors did, in secret.

I was often asked if "Worm" was my family name; and I would always say, "Yes, it was." It was interesting just to watch the questioners' facial expressions. If someone would ask to know my first name, I would always reply, "Book." And they would then know I was simply having some fun. One clever skallywag suggested that my first name should have been "Earth"; and he subsequently asked if I wanted to go fishing with him. "Yes, perhaps later" was my response; but I never did. Yet, my cover had finally been blown. The word spread slowly about my deception. But still, I was accepted as, "Private Worm, the Storyteller."

During an 1865 living history reenactment event, following the assassination of President Lincoln, our Regimental band played *Marching Through Georgia* just to annoy our Rebel reenactors. My Company C comrades and I would usually sing the lyrics loudly and proudly. We all knew this song, by Henry Clay Work and Henry S. Sawyer, was to commemorate General Sherman's decisive March to the Sea (November 15 to December 21, 1864). Then, we would also sing the *National Anthem*. Our general retort to our Rebel possums' complaining was, "To the victors goes the spoils." This is what U.S. Senator Willam Marcy said when referring to Andrew Jackson's 1828 presidential election victory. Perhaps this was somewhat tacky; but quite authentic.

To this day, I always tear up when hearing our *National Anthem*. When a reenacting day was ending, my comrades would sing the Anthem, followed by listening to Taps. One comrade whispered, not so softly into my ear, that if my pitiful voice was to be heard by others, it should be considered as treason. He was probably right. Nevertheless, we all had a good laugh.

A month or so later, my Company C was portraying Union prison guards at Fortress Monroe to ensure the recently captured Jefferson Davis, the former President of the Confederate States of America, could not escape or commit suicide. During this living history event, we all could now relax more easily since any visitor questions could be addressed without any concerns about time sensitivities. This was a huge relief following almost five years to being on your toes every minute of every day during a living history event. During ensuing events, I was often asked to read more of my verses and vignettes. I did so, but these times with a theatrical prop. I pretended to be smoking my 1860's artisanal, long-stemmed, corncob pipe. This seemed to put the listeners into a more receptive frame of mind for some historical fiction.

Once a five-year Civil War anniversary period was over, the planning for the next anniversary period would begin. And I had the privilege to participate in three of those Civil War anniversaries.

But that was then ...

* * *

And now, we come to January 6, 2021. We are now amidst the 160th anniversary (2021-2025) of the American Civil War when a countless number of violent, Confederate flag-waving rioters were among the 10 thousand or so insurrectionists who stormed the Nation's Capital building. I was then, and still am, very angry, sad and horrified. That failed insurrection sought to destroy our nation's Democracy from the inside trying to prevent the peaceful transition of one presidency to another as statutorily mandated in the U.S Constitution. Yet, as of March 2024, only about 14 percent of those actively participating have been legally charged. The events of that treasonous day should serve as a dangerous wake-up call for all Americans. We must all now stay vigilant and proactively engaged. I believe America's future may depend upon it.

In 1992, Billy Ray Cyrus' song of homage, *Some Gave All*, is still powerful and true to this very day. And it's also true that "all gave some." All reenactors know this and will continue to honor all those who did not violate their individual oaths to protect and defend the U.S Constitution and who fought to preserve this sacred Union ... then, now, and into the future.

As Americans, we must not become complacent, complicit, or gullible to those deceptive ideologs who may hide behind the nation's flag to manically convey their intent to establish an insidious kleptocracy that our forefathers fought against. This is now the time to actively stand up for everyone's individual freedoms and rights, and not just for a self-selected few. It's time to vote for our collective future. We must vote to defeat any flag-grasping, revenge-seeking, Confederacy-mongering insurrectionists, who are now aided and abetted by an appeasing U.S. Supreme Court, to legally destroy the foundations of our American democracy. By "all giving some" now, can help prevent "some giving all" later. We do not need to have another American Civil War. Not only would this become another national tragedy, but an unimaginable worldwide tragedy as well. But time will surely tell. These un-American efforts can and must be prevented.

The honorable Ulysses S. Grant, a former Union Army General and the 18th President of the United States, wrote, "If we are to have another contest in the near future of our national existence, I predict that the dividing line will not be the Mason and Dixon's but between patriotism and intelligence on the one side, and superstition, ambition and ignorance on the other."

* * *

To better understand the impact of the American Civil War would be upon our nation today, we only need to extrapolate. In 1860, the population of the United States was about 32 million citizens with this War's nearly 750 thousand causalities; and with today's population of nearly 335 million, that would approximate nearly 8 million American causalities. To put this number into a more recent context, these causalities would be seven-times the number of Covid-19 deaths in the U.S during the 2020-2023 pandemic. This is truly unthinkable.

Historically speaking, this Civil War had more casualties than all the other American wars combined. With the polarization of today's society, could another Civil War occur? I would certainly hope not. Going forward, can future Civil War reenactments be truthfully and forthrightly portrayed? If so, could those reenactments become one means for lessening the political divide? I would certainly hope so.

In 1885, a former Union Army officer, Captain George T. Balch, authored the original text of a *Pledge of Allegiance* that read, "We give our heads and our hearts to God and our country; one country, one language, one flag!" Then, in 1892, the Reverend Francis Bellamy wrote an updated text that would evolve into today's version.

Decades ago, as a youngster in elementary school, I can recall with my right hand over my heart, reciting the latest amended version of the

Pledge of Allegiance. Even at this early age, I believed this shared Pledge was meant "for all," and not just for a self-selected few.

While the American military has its own oath to protect and defend the U.S. Constitution, we too have an oath. So, as citizens, we should collectively reaffirm the immortal words of this patriotic verse: "I pledge allegiance to the Flag of the United States of America and to the Republic for which it stands, one nation under God, indivisible, with liberty and justice for all."

Then on 5 November 2024, enough deceived American voters elected the former President Donald Trump to another term in office. He promised to pardon all insurrectionists who planned and/or attacked the Capitol Building on 6 January 2021 during this "day of love." When fulfilling his campaign promises and initiating many Project 2025 recommendations, will Trump be desecrating the Union forever? Will he be reinstituting some former Confederacy-based precepts? Will he again be violating his Oath of Office? Time will tell."

*So whence dis yankee soldier be endin agin hiz harrowin tales
of dat picket and tator-peeler's futur storytellin saga,
He be furever mor proud of bein dat brave yung privat
still be wearin hiz Union Army blue. Huzzah! Huzzah!*

About the Author

Drew W. Allbritten was an American Civil War reenactor for nearly two decades. He portrayed a young, semi-literate Union soldier; and was involved in dozens of battle scenarios and in scores of living history events.

During a fifty-year career, Dr Drew W. Allbritten was a reforming leader in education and public service. He specialized in leadership and governance, economic and community development, and in education and training at the local, state, national and international levels.

He was the 2021 recipient of the American Association for Adult & Continuing Education's Outstanding Service Medallion (for Lifetime Achievement in advancing the profession).

Drew was a Michigan State Legislator and a Presidential Appointee in HUD's intergovernmental relations office during the Reagan Administration. He also advised officials in other Administrations and served as CEO for non-profit organizations. He has taught and advised South Pacific leaders on a variety of issues related to Public Administration at the University of the South Pacific and Fiji National University. Drew continues to mentor former colleagues and students. He is an advocate for civil rights, social justice and environmental efforts.

Drew has an earned doctorate from Western Michigan University; and most of his professional papers and publications are archived at the Bird Library's Adult Education Special Collections section at Syracuse University (NY). He does some gardening, plays competitive pétanque, and travels internationally. Drew lives in an ancient village in southern France with his wife, Susan Kelly, and their miniature cockapoo, Sydney. If you would like to know more, or make some comments on this book, the author can be reached at *drewallbritten@gmail.com*.

www.hellgatepress.com